UPLOAD YOUR FAITH SERIES

1

THE POWER OF LIFE-GIVING
HOPE
IN
TROUBLESOME TIMES

I0156282

JAY R. ASHBAUCHER

innovo
PUBLISHING

Published by Innovo Publishing, LLC
www.innovopublishing.com
1-888-546-2111

innovo
PUBLISHING

Providing Full-Service Publishing Services for Christian Authors, Artists & Ministries:
Books, eBooks, Audiobooks, Music & Film

THE POWER OF LIFE-GIVING HOPE IN TROUBLESOME TIMES
UPLOAD YOUR FAITH SERIES (BOOK 1)

Scripture taken from the New American Standard Bible® Copyright © 1960, 1962, 1963, 1968, 1971, 1972, 1973, 1975, 1977, 1995 by The Lockman Foundation. Used by permission.

Scripture quotations marked NLT are taken from the Holy Bible, New Living Translation, copyright © 1996, 2004, 2007 by Tyndale House Foundation. Used by permission of Tyndale House Publishers, Inc., Carol Stream, Illinois 60188. All rights reserved.

The Appendix, "The Value of Suffering," was previously published under a separate title: *Out of Darkness Into the Light: Learning to See Life From God's Point of View.*

Library of Congress Control Number: 2018936339
ISBN: 978-1-61314-412-1

Cover Design & Interior Layout: Innovo Publishing, LLC

Printed in the United States of America
U.S. Printing History
First Edition: April 2018

CONTENTS

ACKNOWLEDGING GRATITUDE

To the God of all hope, for his life-giving Word and his Spirit's guidance in this writing.

To my wife, Connie, for some preliminary readings and suggestions, patience with me through many disappearings to work on the project, and her encouraging support.

To my son, Andrew, for critiques and perspectives to consider, and my brother, Reid, for suggestions and technical support.

To the men of my small group who contributed much to my walk with Christ and who continue to influence my thinking and goals.

To my readers for motivation to finish another book of teachings from God's Word.

To Trinity Evangelical Divinity School for giving me a Christian worldview, respect for others' views, and valued training in what it means to be entrusted with the truths of the Bible and the gospel of Jesus (1 Thessalonians 2:4).

To Innovo Publishing and Rachael Carrington, my editor, for much-needed wisdom and help along the way.

INTRODUCTION: WHY THIS BOOK?

UPLOAD YOUR FAITH: WHAT AN ODD SERIES TITLE

This is the first of a planned series of three books, which include uploading your faith with hope, uploading your faith with truth, and uploading your faith with love. I use "Upload Your Faith" as a series title for two reasons—a suggestion from my former men's group and an uploading experience I had with Facebook. During the process of writing a previous book, I shared with my men's group the difficulty I had coming up with a title. After much thoughtfulness and brainstorming, they came up with the title, "Upload Your Faith." I did not use the title because I did not understand uploading and was not sure it fit the intent of the book. But after a recent Facebook experience, I decided to honor my friends by using their suggestion as a series title for three books on the subjects of hope, faith, and love.

I am not a frequent Facebook user, but I do have a Facebook page (or I did last time I looked). One day, thinking my page would be dropped due to years of neglect, I decided to upgrade the page with a different picture of myself. The present picture was blurry and did not portray a very clear likeness. There were three pictures of me on my computer, so I chose one. I then encountered the problem of not knowing how to get it onto my Facebook page. Somehow, in the midst of my keyboard clicking, the word *upload* popped up on the screen. *Hmm,* I thought, *the computer must want me to replace my picture by uploading the new one.* After trying a few keys to see what they would do, in my ignorance, I happened to double-click on the new picture, and to my delight and amazement, the new picture instantly appeared on my Facebook page.

I now see how *upload* can mean upgrading something that is not great with something better. For various reasons, our daily life is often not so great, but God, in the Person of Jesus, provides the complete package of what is great and wants us to replace our tried-and-faltering ways with his far better ways. Jesus says he is the doorway through which we must enter to discover the ultimate abundant and good life (John 10:9-10). To acquire his better life, we must replace the old with something new and better. We need to be on a journey of continuously uploading our faith.

TROUBLESOME TIMES AND HOPESVILLE

Imagine a town named "Hopesville." Hopesville is an inviting and welcoming place. It beckons, "We offer real hope that can change your life and get you through the toughest of times. Come and live here." The inhabitants of Hopesville are recovering from turns for the worse that have plunged their lives into uncertainty, stress, and a search for answers on how to cope. Hopeless people are fearful and worried over what their world is coming to, whether it is their personal lives or the world at large. They are people caught up in addictive habits; people who have lost jobs; people who have finally quit on dreams that never materialized; people who suffer from debilitating and life-threatening health issues; people who are experiencing a failing family life; people whose lives have long been unsatisfying and unhappy; people who are considering suicide; and people who have come to the end of life with a sense of futility and emptiness, having missed what was important to live for.

Hopesville is filled with young people who often use the word *whatever*, which, translated, means "who cares, it doesn't matter." Pleasure seekers come who have figured out there is nothing to live for but to "eat, drink, and be merry, for tomorrow we die." Hopeless people come to Hopesville knowing it's a place where anyone can come to be loved, discover hope, and get a life that can take them on a journey to satisfying places they never imagined possible. You may think you have a fantastic life. But a fantastic life is only defined by your hope and what that hope brings you in the end. Will your hope disappoint you or will it actually happen?

A WORD ABOUT LIFE-GIVING HOPE

If you ask people how they are doing, a standard answer is often "fine" or "good." But many who say these words are not satisfied with their life the way it is and are searching for a new and better way. Many do not realize there is a God of newness. God's message about his newness is communicated in a book called the Bible. Consider these statements: "I create new heavens and a new earth" (Isaiah 65:17); "I will . . . put a new spirit within them" (Ezekiel 11:19); "new wine into fresh wineskins" (Mark 2:22); "a new and living way" (Hebrews 10:20); "a new commandment I give to you . . ." (John 13:34); "I am writing a new commandment to you" (1 John 2:8);[1] "a new creature . . . new things have come" (2 Corinthians 5:17); "I am making all things new" (Revelation 21:5); "Jesus said to him, 'I am the way . . .'" (John 14:6).

Jesus met lots of people who needed a new life. He said to a woman he met, "If you knew the gift of God, and who it is who says to you, 'Give me a drink,' you would have asked Him, and He would have given you living water" (John 4:10). I have a friend, Jim Jensen, who gave me a CD on which is a song called "I Thirst."[2] Some of the lyrics are as follows:

> *One day I came to Him, I was so thirsty,*
> *I asked for water, my throat was so dry . . .*
> *He gave me water that I had never dreamed of,*
> *But for this water He had to die . . .*
> *He said, "I thirst," yet He made the rivers,*
> *He said, "I thirst," yet He made the seas . . .*
> *In His great thirst He brought water to me.*

A man named Saul recognized his need for an upgraded life—actually, not upgraded, but a totally new life, one that would replace his old life. He did not desire this change until he honestly saw what he had become. For Saul to experience a radical transformation in his hopeless life, it took Jesus

1. Some may react to Jesus' words, "a new commandment I give to you." Many of us are not too happy with the word *commandment* because it sounds like we are losing our freedom to be who we are by being controlled by someone else. No one wants that. *I don't like being told what to do* is a sentiment we frequently hear. It may surprise you to know that God does not want that for us. He has created each of us to be unique, with varying gifts, talents, interests, and personalities. He wants us to be who He originally designed us to be. God's way is a way of freedom (John 8:31-32; Galatians 5:1, 13). In my previous book, *Out of Darkness into the Light*, I explain how freedom works in a chapter titled "Is Christianity a Religion of Do's and Don'ts?" It helps us gain insight and understanding concerning freedom from dos and don'ts.

2. Beverly Lowrey, "I Thirst" (Lyrics © BMG Rights Management US, LLC). The words *I thirst* come from a statement Jesus made during his sufferings on the cross (John 19:28). Cp. John 7:37-39.

appearing to him, speaking truth to him, and physically blinding him. We can read about it in the Bible (Acts 9:1-30). Because many of us, like Saul, fail to see our lives for what they are, we too need certain events to humble us (to create a sense of hopelessness) so we will seek a change. Saul became a new man. New life was uploaded—that is, transferred—from Jesus into Saul. The picture of who he was as Saul was exchanged for a new one: he became the Apostle Paul. Subsequent growth in his new-found life is explained by him in Philippians 3:4-14 and 1 Timothy 1:13-16.

As a result of this newly implanted life, he now found himself on an exciting new journey—but one in which he possessed two natures that were in conflict with each other: the old self and the new self (Ephesians 4:22-24). His goal was to replace the old with the new, like when I uploaded a new Facebook picture to replace my old one (Romans 7:14-8:17). If we as believers will continually upload our faith by understanding and growing in God's grace and knowledge (2 Peter 1:3-11; 3:18), we will find ourselves replacing the picture of who we were with who we are in Christ Jesus. Without getting a life from the life-giver, it is impossible to know how fantastic life can really be, even in the midst of the most severe sufferings. Many are fearful of what this world is coming to. The world is being seriously threatened by evils. Our potential sufferings are unimaginable. This book is written to explain how new life comes to us and what real hope means in light of what God says our world is coming to.

A NOTE ABOUT THE APPENDIX

When people go through troublesome times, they experience various degrees of suffering. Many have questions about suffering, including why God continues to allow suffering in this world. I felt the book needed a discussion on the subject to answer a few questions and to help readers see how God is able to use our sufferings for good. Rather than write another chapter, I decided to include, as an appendix, what I have already written elsewhere.

At this point, let me also say a word about the scripture references throughout the book. They allow the reader to check out what the Bible says on the subject being put forth. What God says to us is more important than what I say. The scripture references allow for good small group discussion. A guide for groups of two or more is in the back of the book (Matthew 18:20).

CHAPTER 1

THE MEANING AND IMPORTANCE OF HOPE

M ost of us do not want to suffer, but no matter how minimal or severe, it is something we must learn how to do. Hilda Born, in her book *Walking with Hope*,[3] shares a personal story. At twenty-five years old, she was diagnosed with acute rheumatoid arthritis. After three months in the hospital, she felt completely hopeless and discouraged and was finally sent home to live life in a wheelchair. "The way I saw it," she says, "the prudent thing for God to do was to let me die. It certainly wasn't fair to ask my husband to care for a crippled wife and three young children. Of course, I bargained with God, 'If you heal me I will do this and this, but mostly I pledge to help the helpless.'" Hilda felt helpless, depressed, and imprisoned in a hopeless situation. She did eventually walk again, but at the time, she needed a hope to help her endure her sufferings. She learned to "walk with hope."

Generations of people from ancient times have wrestled with the problem of suffering and have responded to their sufferings in various ways. Some decide there must be no God or he would do away with suffering. Many think they are on their own in this world. They just tough

---

3. Jacob and Hilda Born, *Walking with Hope and Thoughts Along the Way* (Abbotsford, B. C.: Canada Imprint Press Publishers, 2002).

it out and do the best they can. Others get mad at God and will have nothing more to do with him. Still others are disappointed that God has not answered their prayers, and depression or despair overwhelms them. But there are some who have come to know and understand enough about God to be enabled to overcome anxiety, unbelief, anger, disappointment, or despair, and walk with God-given hope.

HOPE DEFINED

Upon reviewing a variety of dictionaries, I arrived at the following definitions of hope: In noun form, hope is *an object, person, or event* that you are counting on to make things turn out all right. In verb form, hope is a feeling that what is wanted or longed for will happen; *a desire* accompanied by anticipation or expectation; to expect something with confidence. Thus we see that hope is both an object (objective) and a feeling or desire (subjective). Objectively, hope sees what is up ahead. Subjectively, hope is focusing on and desiring what is up ahead. Therefore, hope is the knowledge or content of what is ahead, which supplies a desire to press on toward it.

There are three different kinds of hope: false hope, probable hope, and true hope. All of these help us persevere in life's trials, but the end results will be different.

1. *False hope* is based on things that are not true and will therefore disappoint us in the end. If we put our hope in lies, they will fail to give what they promise. The object of hope must be true and real in order for it to happen as expected. I can believe and hope in a prescribed pill to cure me of an ailment, but if I unknowingly take the wrong pill, my hope for a cure will not happen.

2. *Probable hope* is based on reasonable possibilities. I may have good reason to hope that it will not rain next Saturday so I can go fishing or golfing, or I can hope with confidence that things will work out in my troubled family life, or that my problems at work will be resolved, or that God will answer my prayers—but that does not mean things will turn out as I want. Expecting that what I hope for

will happen is merely probable because it may or may not happen. The end is in doubt until we see what happens.

3. *True hope* gives us confidence that our expectation will be met because it is based on what we know will happen. Some might think, *How can that kind of hope exist? No one knows the future for certain.* The Bible presents a God who knows and tells the truth about the future and who has the power to make it happen. It is on this basis that we who are indwelt by Christ feel absolutely certain about what will happen, and it will not disappoint us (Romans 5:5).

Each of these three kinds of hope help sustain us by giving encouragement that things can or will get better, but only trusted biblical hope is the kind that leaves no doubt. Notice, I said *trusted* hope.

I need to say a word about faith, which means trusting. Faith is different from hope. Hope is yet unseen, but by faith we know it will eventually happen. Faith is what tells you that your expected promise from God is a sure thing; you can count on it one hundred percent, whereas hope is the sure thing itself. Faith means knowing and trusting God's promised hope will be fulfilled. As the Bible says, "Now faith is the assurance of things hoped for, the conviction of things not seen" (Hebrews 11:1). Hebrews 11 is about faith, but when you study it, you have to ask, faith in what? That *what* in which we place our confident faith consists of God's promises, things that are yet unseen—in other words, our hope. For example, God promised Abraham a future land—yes, an earthly one, but beyond that, a heavenly one. Abraham died in faith, not having received the earthly promise or the heavenly one, but he saw them and knew they would come.

In Hebrews 11 we learn that faith in God brought rewarding blessings to lots of people, but many with faith suffered persecutions, anywhere from mocking to horrible death. But whether good happened to them in this life or bad, they all looked forward to their future. For their faith was in the hope of what God promised, and all who believe, including us, will share in those same promises (Hebrews 11:32-40). Hope is not something we conjure up; rather, hope is something God reveals to us. And when we believe it, we are helped to persevere in times of suffering or to patiently wait in times of uncertainty.

It is important to know that hope does not mean sitting back, doing nothing, and hoping for future things to happen. Rather, the expectation of what's coming requires us to prepare and get ready for what's coming, and in the interim, to live life each day as God means for it to be lived.

THE MEANING AND IMPORTANCE OF HOPE

High up in the mountains, melting snow creates the beginnings of rushing streams and flowing rivers. The water at these beginnings has not yet met conditions for much contamination and is drinkable, and it is *mmm* good and especially refreshing after a hot and exhausting hike to get there.

For a number of years, I would take a group of kids in grades 4–6 on a summer hike in the mountains of Montana. When the kids wanted to give up and quit, especially during the steeper parts, I would encourage them with words like, "you can do it," "c'mon, just one step at a time," "it's not very far now," "toughing it out will help you tough out other hard things that come along in your life." But especially, I would keep reminding them of my promise that at the top would be the reward of a grand spectacular view, a time to rest our bodies, and the refreshing satisfaction of drinking cool water. I would say, "It will be an amazing experience, and you don't want to miss it," and the words of what to expect up ahead encouraged me too.

There were always kids who wanted to drop out and sit down until the rest of us returned, but sticking together and helping each other, we all made it. The greatest temptations to quit came during their times of tiredness and weakness, and it is at those times we are susceptible to making potentially devastating decisions. The ability to endure through the hard times often requires us to remind ourselves and be excited about the promised good that is up ahead—to be encouraged that we have what it takes to get there. Hope believed helps us to endure our hardships because the reward for getting there is too amazing to miss.

Suffering is far from easy and can cause us to despair in life. In the movie *The Lord of the Rings*, one of the characters is sitting with Gandalf, knowing that he is soon to be killed by enemies. He says, "I didn't think life would end this way." Gandalf answers, "End? No, life does not end here." He goes on to explain a life that continues beyond death. This hopeful message comforts his fearful friend because he can look forward to something good, real, and ongoing. Not only that, but it gave him courage to re-enter his present battle, hoping for victory, knowing that the final outcome would not be the end of all if it did not turn out as he wanted.

Whenever we feel our lives spinning out of control, we need hope. It is frustrating, despairing, and dangerous to our well-being to have lost all hope—to be in a place of not knowing what to do or where to turn. One of the saddest statements in the Bible is that people live in this world without God and without hope (Ephesians 2:12). Hope restores our thinking to a positive outlook and enables us to experience the joy of knowing that everything will be all right, no matter what the situation (Psalm 62:5-6). A biblical psalm writer has learned to walk with hope. He prays to God, *remind me of your word* "in which You have made me hope. This is my comfort in my affliction that your word has revived me" (Psalm 119:49-50).

Where Hope Comes From

Christian hope begins with God, not with us. Unless God provides something, there is little or nothing to hope for. He is the God of hope (Romans 15:13).

Israel has many stories of men and women God used to rescue them from afflictions that threatened their well-being and their existence. But when each of these heroic men and women died, Israel again found themselves in adverse and oppressing situations and in need of another one to save them. God gave Israel the hope of a coming Messiah, who like their other saviors would also die, but unlike the others would be raised from the dead, never to die again (Psalm 2:7; 16:10; Acts 13:32-37). This Messiah would be their Savior from all threats, promising a glorious future.

In addition, because the people of Israel were the primary cause of their own downfalls, constantly rebelling against God and going away from him, God promised to give them a new heart so they could love God and faithfully live a life in union with God's design for them

(Jeremiah 31:31-34; Ezekiel 36:22-28). Furthermore, this promised Messiah (Christ) would offer this same hope of a new heart to all people, everywhere (Genesis 12:1-3; Galatians 3:8-9; Luke 2:25-32). The Bible says God *causes* us "to be born again to a *living hope* through the resurrection of Jesus Christ from the dead" (1 Peter 1:3). God's new life and hope comes into reality for us when we trust God's Word (1 Peter 1:23, 25).

God caused this living hope to become a reality in my life due to my fear of death. I was panic stricken—totally hopeless—because I knew I was going to die, and nothing could be done to prevent it. The world is full of cemeteries where the dead are buried, and no one comes out. But when I heard the message about Jesus being *the resurrection and the life* and that *if I believed in him I would never die* (John 11:25-26), it instantly became the answer I desperately needed to hear. Jesus was the person I needed in my life. Immediately I found myself believing in him and his Word. In fact, even though I may not have realized it at the time, I was now committed to following him the rest of my life because there was no one else who could give me the life I longed for.

When I gladly accepted this message of Jesus as my life-giver, something happened within me. A relieved feeling came over me, and I went from hopelessness to being a person with hope. Now, even if I die physically, I will still live in the presence of Jesus and one day be bodily resurrected. Knowing I will never die, there was a feeling of peace and joy. As I grew in my understanding, I came to see that a pattern given in the Bible was the pattern that took place in my life. At first I did not know this God who had the answer to my hopeless situation. All I knew was that something within me was crying out to live and not die. "Whoever will call on the name of the Lord will be saved" (Romans 10:13). But how could I call on him in whom I had not believed, and how could I believe if I had not heard, and how could I hear without a messenger delivering the message (Romans 10:14)? God sent a messenger (my mother) to tell me this life-giving good news of who Jesus was and what he could do for me. "So faith comes by hearing, and hearing by the word of Christ" (Romans 10:17).

When I heard the good news that Jesus could give me his eternal life (which is not just a future life but a quality of life now), my disturbed and longing heart called out to God, "Yes, Lord, I need and want this gift of life." I found myself believing in Jesus and his Word and was no longer a scared, anxiety-filled, hopeless person. God caused me to be born again, which brought forth a living hope inside of me. Jesus was that living hope. His Spirit came into me, and just as Jesus was raised from the dead, so shall I be. Furthermore, his coming into me began the process of my becoming like he is (1 John 3:2).

God cares about all of us. He loves us and wants a relationship with us. You may have a disturbing, felt need or longing different from mine, but the same God offers you the same pathway back to him, leading to the same hope. When the opportunity arises, what will you choose? He is the living hope who unites all believers into a newly created human family, a family that will continue on in the new age and world to come. We are his people, and he is our God (1 Peter 2:9-10).

What do many people have as their hope for a satisfying life and a better world? Here are some examples of false or probable hopes. Some hope in the philosophy of evolution; life is evolving, and our world will get better and better with time. But who knows where evolution is going to end up? Some hope in the advancing technologies of science—amazing technologies that are helping us daily, or ones that will be discovered, possibly with the answer to aging and death. Yes, we can thankfully hope in present technologies, even to cure us of ill health, but unfortunately, science (in many areas), as much as it has been a good thing, cannot guarantee all it promises, and science does not deal with some matters that are outside its realm. Some people put their hope in politics—that mankind will eventually get it together and create a peaceful world. But, from early on in human history, wars have existed, and by the looks of things, they are not likely to end. In fact, the Bible reports that only by the coming of Christ Jesus to bring his kingdom on earth will there be an all-encompassing peaceful world (Isaiah 9:6-7; Daniel 7:13-14, 18; Luke 1:30-33). People also put their hopes in education, or in their abilities, or in their own wishful thinking, or in various religious beliefs. Some people hope in mind over matter and would tell us that suffering and evil only exist in our mind and that we can ignore evils and create our own reality. Or they hope in positive thinking: *believe the best in yourself, and all will turn out OK.*

The truth is, evil, suffering, and death are a reality of this world, and it hinders what we hope for. Although we can trust in many of humankind's achievements and promises, the Bible warns us not to put our ultimate hope in anything that originates from human efforts or religions (Psalm 146:3-7; Jeremiah 17:5). True hope takes as its object Jesus and all he offers and promises.

CONTENT OF CHRISTIAN HOPE

What does Jesus offer? Many are familiar with the word *inheritance.* We "will" to give our possessions to family members who survive us. Sometimes family members fight over what they want—this is not good. A family member once asked Jesus to serve as a referee and tell his brother to divide the inheritance with him. Jesus took the opportunity to warn people about greed. In this world we continually want more stuff. Jesus responded that even if we have all the *stuff* we want, *life* does not consist of possessions (Luke 12:13-15). Even so, we do have an inheritance from the Lord (Romans 8:16-17, 32).

The Bible mentions a few things that God's children can expect as part of their inheritance. Some of them may be things most of us have not thought about. For example, we inherit a blessing (1 Peter 3:9). In Old Testament days, children looked forward to a blessing from their fathers (Genesis 28:1-4). Since God is our Father, we inherit his blessing (Genesis 26:24-29). Jesus, representing the Father, gives out blessings to all who believe in him. God's blessings refer to good things we can expect. For example, "Blessed are you when people insult you and persecute you, and falsely say all kinds of evil against you because of Me. Rejoice and be glad, for *your reward in heaven is great*" (Matthew 5:11-12). To those who suffer deep pain from the loss of loved ones, or perhaps other losses, Jesus said, "Blessed are those who mourn, for *they shall be comforted*" (Matthew 5:4). What a wonderful blessing it is to inherit comfort after all we have suffered. One of those comforts is *being reunited with loved ones* (1 Thessalonians 4:13-18).

One other blessing I will mention is that those who are genuinely humble and meek in God's eyes but are thought to be weak in human eyes are blessed, for *they shall inherit the earth* (Matthew 5:5). I leave it to you to look up and study the things we inherit, both present and future (Matthew 19:29; Romans 4:13-14; Hebrews 6:11-12; Revelation 21:1-7). Many details about the Christian hope will be given in chapter six of this book.

How do we become heirs of all God wills to give us? By his mercy and great love, he enables us to become his family and thus heirs of his kingdom (John 1:10-13; Romans 8:15-17; Galatians 4:4-7). God took the initiative to make us his children. *He*, not us, sent Jesus to be the Savior of the world; *he,* not us, willed for Christ Jesus to suffer persecution and death on a cross to make it possible for us to inherit salvation; *he*, not us, raised Jesus from the dead to assure us of Christ's divine identity and power to save us; *he,* not us, sent us the message (the Bible) by his Son and apostles that tells us why we should and how we can be saved; *he*, not us, calls us to himself; *he*, not us, convicts our hearts of the need to respond to his saving message; *he*, not us, gives the gift of eternal life to all who repent, believe, and are baptized into Christ; and *he*, not us, gives the gift of his Holy Spirit, by which we are adopted into God's family and guaranteed a life in his kingdom. Blessed are you, O God, the Father of our Lord Jesus Christ. We praise you. We would have zero hope without your mercy; thank you, Father, for loving us and making possible our salvation. You have given us a living hope, which is the anchor of our souls in troublesome times (Hebrews 6:17-19).

QUESTIONS ABOUT HOPE

Is hope only in the distant future, or is there hope for now? If we hope in God for daily help, does that hope find its fulfillment in the present? God came into our world to show us his love and his power in the Person of God the Son. Jesus allowed us to get a glimpse of God's kingdom and God's character by things he said and did when he walked on the earth. Those who put faith in Christ Jesus are transferred into the kingdom of God's dear Son and are now living on this earth as citizens of his kingdom (Colossians 1:13). We are Jesus' feet, hands, and heart, and the work we do in the name of Jesus reveals something of God's kingdom in the present.

God is compassionate and merciful, and he satisfies the hopes of hurting people through those who learn from him (Matthew 25:34-40). He gave us spiritual gifts to bring healing and help to others (1 Corinthians 12:25-31). Thus a partial fulfilling of the hope of God's future kingdom blessings is here now. If the poor are lacking food and trusting that God will meet their need, when we hear their cry and bring food to them, we, as God's representatives, are the fulfillment of their hope (Proverbs 22:9; Isaiah 41:17). Whenever any of us is praying and trusting for help, our hope in God is often fulfilled by God's directing someone to us. For those who have messed up their lives and long for new life, we are Christ's messengers of hope (Matthew 9:36-38; Acts 26:16-18). Present hope includes the truth that he is always with us, never leaving or forsaking us (Hebrews 13:5), and that he often appears in unexpected ways to help us in whatever our situation. We make our requests known to him and trust his goodness, expectantly looking forward to what he will do and accepting whatever that might be. God often hears our prayers and acts on our behalf. In these ways, hope is fulfilled in our daily lives.

Admittedly, when we pray, we do not always know what God will do. Many people experience tragedy instead of protection. Those times are so disruptive and disorienting that there is no immediate hope or comfort. In those times of deep pain and anguish in which we cry out, *Why, God, did you allow this to happen?* one can only suffer through such grief until hope can be restored. Often all that we can hope for is to trust God's Word, which says, "And we know that God causes all things to work together for good to those who love God, to those who are called according to His purpose" (Romans 8:28). Even then, in our grief, this word of hope is not acceptable. At times our only comfort may be the knowledge that the God we believe in is all wise and good and that he has a sufficient reason for allowing evil things to happen. Even though we may not know God's reason for allowing such suffering, the Bible has much to say about the value of suffering and the good that can come out of it. We can gain from the benefits of suffering (see the appendix of this book), but we may have to look for our ultimate comfort in God's promised hope to be fulfilled when his kingdom comes in all its fullness.

When people talk about future hope, it's easy to say, "I don't care about the future, I care about living my life now." OK, but it's a mistake to think that hope does not affect the now. How we live each day—and what we live for—is based on ever-present hope. When our hope is gone, it's easy to lose our way, despair, and give up on today's life and goals. Here is a story to show what I mean. In the movie *Nanny McPhee Returns*, a mother of three young kids fights hard against all odds to keep their farm afloat while her husband is away at war. Her hope is that her husband will return and everything will be all right. When she receives a false report that he was killed, she loses all hope, gives up trying to save the farm, and is determined to sell it. Fortunately, her husband, who was injured and reported as missing, unexpectedly comes home. Her spirits are lifted and her purpose for everyday living returns. Her hope is what gave her what she needed to endure life's hardships. Hope gave her life meaning and purpose, and it directed how she lived each day. If you asked her why she worked so hard to save the farm, she would have said, "My husband will be back, and I can't give up and lose what we have worked for. He's expecting it to be here for him when he returns."

What is your hope? We all have a hope that provides our reason for living. The problem is, we live in a world that is not always reliable, and if what we hope for is lost, so is our purpose for living. If the object of our hope is false or is something that fails us (health, money, family, job), our spirits are dashed until we can gain something else to hope for. Temporal or worldly hopes cannot always be trusted to be there. But if we have a hope that is certain and cannot be destroyed, when life throws us a curve, we can endure because our purpose for living revolves around eternal perspectives and directives. We keep going because we are living for a guaranteed hope, which always provides us a purpose and goal for day-to-day living. We should care about the future, particularly the hope that drives us. Think about it. What hope gives you your *why* for living each day? Is that hope reliable?

APPLYING HOPE WHEN NEEDED

In the midst of our suffering, God says, "Fix your hope completely on the grace to be brought to you at the revelation of Jesus Christ" (1 Peter 1:13). The word *fix* means to perfectly, fully, and completely focus on your hope. When in the midst of troublesome situations, we must learn to intentionally change our thinking from what is bothering us to thinking about the things Jesus has promised us. We are to be "fixing our eyes on Jesus, the author and perfecter of faith, who for the joy set before Him endured the cross" (Hebrews 12:2). The phrase *fixing our eyes* means to view with undivided attention by looking away from every other object and focusing earnestly on Jesus and the joy he sets before us. What Jesus saw gave him joy and enabled him to endure the sufferings of the cross. Joy and endurance to get through our hardship comes by training ourselves to focus on our hope in the midst of our trial.

I have often thought about and wondered how David, past great king of Israel, strengthened himself when faced with being stoned by his angry comrades (1 Samuel 30:1-8). A clue comes to me in a psalm he wrote: "Surely I have composed and quieted my soul . . . like a weaned child within me. O Israel, hope in the Lord" (Psalm 131:2-3). David thinks about an upset and fussing child being tended to by a loving mother and how the child's weaned soul is at rest and content. Likewise, when we bring ourselves into the presence of God and focus on his love and care, on his promises, and on all the ways he has helped us in the past, we become peaceful and content. David's ability to gain strength and overcome his dire circumstances and sufferings grew as he communed with God, experienced his presence, and remembered his faithfulness. Out of his weakness and trust came peace and contentment, which made David invincible. He tells Israel to put their hope in the Lord, for such hope gives strength to move back into the struggle. Ask for God's wisdom, and do what God says to do.

In times of depressing trials, there needs to be a conscious effort to change our thinking and focus. Knowing the content of our hope gives us the right object to focus on. When faced with sufferings and even persecutions, as a believer in Jesus, imagine meeting him and being with him, and imagine what he has promised you in his Word. Let it bring joy to your heart, leading to the patient endurance of your sufferings.

You may have heard it expressed that Jesus never promised us a life of ease and freedom from troubles, but he did promise to go through them with us and to bless us with his awesome presence. Stephen was among the first martyrs who suffered extreme persecution for faith in Christ. He had trusted Jesus to be his Savior and Lord. One day he found himself being falsely judged, angrily accused, and condemned to die. Instead of Jesus protecting him and making his life go smoothly, he found himself being unjustly battered by a barrage of hurled rocks. But in the midst of his suffering, hope broke in on his moments of cruel affliction.

Sometimes God surprises us with hope. That hope was a vision of Jesus appearing in the heavens, convincing Stephen that he was not abandoned and that the life Jesus promised was real. Hope was a gracious and timely gift from God that enabled Stephen to endure his sufferings. In the midst of his suffering, with the comfort of hope in his heart, Stephen forgave his enemies and fell asleep (Acts 7:54-60). In his time of death, Stephen saw his hope. Like Stephen, those who trust their lives into his care will never die. Jesus is our hope of resurrection and glory (1 Timothy 1:1; see also John 11:25-26; Acts 23:6; Colossians 1:27).

Dale E. Galloway tells about a contractor who was building a levee along a riverbank. A great storm and flood came that buried all of his earth-moving machinery and destroyed the work that he had been doing. After the water receded, his workers were standing around surveying the situation, despondently looking at the mud and the buried machinery. The boss asked them why it was that they looked so gloomy. They responded, "Don't you see what has happened? Our machinery is covered with mud."

"What mud?"

"What mud?" they exclaimed. "Look around you. It is a sea of mud."

"Oh," said the contractor, "I don't see any mud because I am looking at a clear blue sky, and there is no mud up there. There is only sunshine, and I never saw any mud that could stand against sunshine. Soon it will be all dried up, and then you will be able to move your machinery and start up again." His workers had lost hope, but the contractor looked beyond the problem to a certainty that provided hope.[4] Learn to walk with hope. Though I may be tired by the length of my road, I will not say it is hopeless. I choose to trust in the Lord (Jeremiah 17:7), be encouraged by God's Word (Romans 15:4), and be sustained by my blessed hope (Titus 2:11-14).

---

4.   Dale E. Galloway, *12 Ways to Develop a Positive Attitude* (Wheaton: Tyndale, 1975), 26-27.

CHAPTER 2

WHAT'S THE WORLD COMING TO? WHAT IS OUR HOPE?

M ost of us live from day to day in our own busy world, a world much to our own making, occupied by the daily events that matter to us and in which we feel pretty much unaffected by what's going on in the larger world around us. Sure, we have our problems, but nothing we can't handle with the help of our surrounding support systems. But many who have lived a few decades more than others have noticed changes. The world has become much different than it was. Changes have been happening fast, not only in communication technology, medicine, education, and economics, but in the ways people behave toward one another.

Changes are to be expected, but when it appears that those changes have produced a downturn in society, a sudden thought may flash across people's minds—something like, *What's the world coming to?* They shake their heads in disbelief or disgust and then continue on with their daily routines, unaffected by the bigger world—at least unaffected for now. The question that forms this chapter's title crosses their minds because, to them, the fast-changing world they are caught up in seems to be getting worse instead of better.

This is nothing new, as people throughout history have thought the same. Conflicts, pain, suffering, troubles, fears, wars, and insecurities abound, preventing personal peace and safety. Concerned people ask, "Is there any hope for a worry-free, evil-free, disease-free, peaceful future for my life, my family, and for our world? From where will such a hope come?"

For some people there is a hopeful side. I hear them say things like, "I was at a charity event, and I met the nicest people. They were all friendly, good people who want to help others. My faith in the goodness of people was restored." What I hear them saying is they always hear about the bad stuff going on in the world, but there are tons of good people out there who give them hope that the world will become a better place. Even though I admire the same goodness in people, the question remains: What is the world coming to?

What is our hope for a better world? When you think about it, there are two primary answers: humans will create the world to be a place of love, peace, and happiness, or there is a Creator God who we must trust to bring it about. When you first read this chapter title, and with this being a book on the Christian hope we have through Christ, some may think, *Oh no! Not another prediction of Jesus' coming and the end of the world. Don't bother me with those religious views.* I understand that concern. I still remember reading a book describing eighty-eight reasons Jesus will come in 1988, and yet nothing happened in 1988. Even though I have my views on end-of-the-world events, date setting and a finely detailed presentation of this subject is not what this chapter is about. Personally, I am convinced there is one God who created all things, who cares about our world, and who has given us biblical prophesies of what he knows is coming and what he intends to do. Later in this chapter we shall consider some of them. Is the fulfilment of those prophesies what the world is coming to? If so, the question of what the world is coming to can be answered with a degree of certainty. Why? Because if the answer comes from the God revealed in the Bible, such a God has the power to make it happen. But as I mentioned above, there is another side to this question. There is a way of life adopted by many that says we humans can bring about a world of peace, harmony, and goodness. The question is, can humanistic efforts promise to bring in a new and better world? Or is there a God, often working through humans, who determines and guarantees a new and better world?

HUMAN VIEWS OF THE COMING WORLD AND OUR HOPE

I would like to begin by defining and addressing viewpoints of those who believe humans can bring about a good world. I am indebted to the philosophy of humanism as a beginning place for defining what humans believe. The goal of those who adopt this philosophy is to promote the preservation and well-being of the human race by defining human values and working toward their implementation. Humanism looks at life strictly from a human point of view.

In 1933 a group of thirty-four humanists met together to discuss and define humanist ideals. Forty years later, humanists again got together to broaden their horizons and improve on their definitions. Each of those meetings resulted in a document. Those documents are circulated today as *Humanist Manifestos I and II. Manifesto 2000* has been added, and more may come. These manifestos are available for all to read (via the Internet or booklet), and I recommend their reading. Humanists are concerned that this world would become the best it can be, and they do an excellent job of providing a well thought-out philosophy on what humans can do to make it happen. From a strictly human point of view, *and if there were no God*, I would say the kind of world humanists envision and are working to see happen sounds like an ideal world to live in.

What do many humanists believe? Humanists believe that we humans can exercise great goodness, and with our intelligence and reasoning skills, we can accomplish the kind of world where happiness, peace, unity, prosperity, and safety thrive. High on the list of hopes for creating a better world is science. With its many discoveries, science will continue to increase our understanding of how the world works, and through many new inventions and beneficial products, the well-being of society will be enhanced. We humans owe our future good to the ongoing progress of science. Science will provide solutions for many present-day needs and future problems. Without lessening the value of the arts, humans are daily relying on scientific endeavors for their health care, communication systems, travel, comforts, and pleasures. Life is good because of science, and it will get better. Genetic engineering promises to be a rising star for hopes of a better world, claiming to be able to eliminate or fix human problems—for example, preventing birth defects or curbing anger.

Some scientists provide the basis for those who believe we can achieve a good world without God. Those scientists say the world was not created by any god, that material substance has always existed, and out of that substance all things have, and still are, evolving into all that makes up the world. It is claimed that the scientific method used for discovering what is real finds no evidence for the existence of God. There is no evidence for an immaterial world consisting of spirit, soul, or life after death. Convinced we live in a completely physical universe, non-theists reasonably believe there is no God to help us and that hope for a better world must come from humans alone.

In addition to human goodness and science, another facet humanists have for making the world a better place requires a proper view of religion. There is a place for religion in society because of valuable moral teachings and practices that can better individuals' lives. However, many religious beliefs, especially in traditional religions, are preventing progress toward a better world. They do not fit in with changing cultural values. Traditional religion is not in tune with current views on tolerance and new-age truth that are necessary for living in a pluralistic society. Freedom of religion must be allowed for all, but religions must not push their values on the world; therefore, separation of church and state is essential, including a reduction of religious influence in public places. For many humanists, some religions have proved to be uninviting, judgmental, and repressive, and with a history of committing atrocities in the name of their gods, they cannot be trusted to help make our world a better place.

Regarding compassion for others, humans have learned through studies and experience what enhances good relationships and what doesn't. Humans have progressed in psychological and sociological sciences and are quite capable of identifying and counseling personal problems and helping others achieve mental and emotional stability, thus providing hope for the betterment of humankind. Also, abundant and varied humanitarian efforts are demonstrating that humans have the goodness and compassion it takes to help hurting people and meet the needs of the world's poor.

Education serves a very important role for instilling the ideals of humanism into the minds of society's future citizens and world leaders. Humans are to encourage tolerance and acceptance of self-chosen lifestyles and varying sexual orientations, so long as these do not endanger or hurt anyone. Humans are encouraged to respect individual rights and promote freedom of choice (within proper boundaries). All levels of society should be democratic in the sense of allowing everyone a voice in what things would best enhance their own life and the lives of fellow humans. Persons are encouraged to be committed to peace, prosperity, and happiness for all humankind, working together to make the world a better place.

Governments are the "go to" problem-solvers and suppliers for its citizens' needs. Because the world is more interconnected due to technology, communication, business, and travel, whatever one nation does impacts other parts of the world in greater ways than ever before. Humans also recognize there are worldwide problems like economics, hunger, and differing political ideologies. Many humanists agree that war is no longer a viable option for solving our problems; we must learn to communicate and work toward peaceful solutions. The solving of world issues will undoubtedly require working toward some form of a worldwide governing body.

Humanists have many admirable views and goals that Christians can agree with. We wish for many of the same things. It is good to want to build a world where we can communicate about our problems and rid ourselves of war. It is good to promote the growth of technology that will benefit people. It is good to teach a morality that would make for good behavior and help restrain people from hurting themselves and others. It is good to be properly respectful and tolerant of one another. It is good to get wise counseling for mental and emotional problems. It is good for the human race to use good reasoning and take responsibility to work together toward a better world.

When I take a close look at humanistic ideals and look at what is happening in the world around me, my impression is that these ideals are increasingly defining today's world. Humanistic ideals appear to have the leading influence in determining the evolving direction of our world. We notice them in many present-day movements, including liberalism, atheism, Darwinian evolution, proposals for a one-world government, separation of church and state, and a growing secularism largely indifferent to God and religion. Humanistic ideals, knowingly or unknowingly, are promoted through secular universities, grade schools, radio news programs, TV, movies, printed and social media, political agendas, and government programs. Yes, humanistic and secular thinking is increasingly becoming our world's way of life and our hope for a better world.[5]

Here is an example of one way humanistic ideals are promoted. I like movies, but I often find myself analyzing them. Someone once asked me, "Why must you philosophize about movies? Why not simply enjoy them for what they are?" Most movies I do enjoy for what they are, but one reason for philosophizing is that I see movies as an art form that, like other art forms, reflects what is happening in our surrounding culture. Besides, I think philosophers help us think about things we would normally not think about.

So here I go analyzing again. I chose one of the popular *Ice Age* movies because it deals with the subject of what their world is coming to. It is fun, thrilling, and entertaining. It is about how the creatures overcome their fears of a speeding meteor hurtling through space—on target to bring their world to an end. It portrays a variety of ordinary characters we can identify with in everyday life. How did they solve their fearful, world-ending problem? They listened to an educated leader who helped them understand scientific principles; then, by working together, they applied those principles to their situation. Their planet is saved, and fears are alleviated by human ingenuity and cooperation.

Movie producers may not intentionally promote humanistic beliefs, but this movie nevertheless shows how many of humanism's

---

5. An interesting opposing assessment of humanism's potential can be read in David Ehrenfeld, *The Arrogance of Humanism* (Oxford University Press, 1978, 1981). As an American professor of biology at Rutgers University, he has authored numerous books, including *Swimming Lessons: Keeping Afloat in the Age of Technology,* and is founding editor of a scientific journal that deals with conserving the biodiversity of Earth.

ideals are taking hold in our world. For example, *without the help of any God, by our own wisdom and goodness, we can save ourselves.* In the movie this saving comes through characters that are shown to be able to overcome doubts, poor attitudes, and negative behaviors and finally work together as friends, even as enemies, cooperating for the common good.

Another humanistic ideal illustrated in the film is the value and ability of sound human reasoning as the best way to attack our problems. The movie includes religion, and though respectfully tolerated, it is portrayed as irrelevant and uninvolved in answers to the *real* survival and preservation of the human race. True, many of these ideals presented in the film are believed by Christians as well, and my point is not that movies need to include a God worldview to be of value but only that the values of humanism are increasingly, even unknowingly, coming to the forefront in people's way of thinking and living. Many if not a large majority of people today could read the humanist manifestos and think, *Yeah, I agree with all of that. What's the problem?*

It's valuable to see a comparison of human views alongside God's because it gives opportunity to assess which views we think are wise to adopt. Let me be clear about my view of human ideals and potential. I do not downplay human abilities or greatness. It was God who said about us humans that we were created in his holy image, and we were created good (Genesis 1:26-27, 31). It was God who charged and entrusted humans with the care and enjoyment of the world he made for them (Genesis 1:28; 2:15). It was God who created us to care for each other (Genesis 4:6-11; 1 John 4:20-21). Even after we fell away from God, with our resulting human imperfections, God has implied that whatever humans can imagine and purpose to do is likely to meet with a great degree of success (Genesis 11:6; Ecclesiastes 2:4-10).

In no way do I wish to discredit or minimize that we humans have accomplished great, good, and amazing things in all areas of life, nor do I discredit that there is goodness in each of us. Good deeds are exhibited in the world every day by Christians and non-Christians alike. As followers of the Lord Jesus who are being recreated and restored to the image of God, we have a responsibility to be zealous in practicing good deeds toward all people (Galatians 6:9-10; Titus 2:14). Christians believe in human goodness because God put his goodness into all of us when he created us in his image. But as long as evil is ever present in and around each of us, no one person or group can guarantee humanistic ideals; and this is why we need a savior. Will that savior be humans, or must we rely on God to bring about a peaceful, prosperous, and unified world? The question remains, *What is the world coming to, and what is our hope?*

GOD'S VIEWS OF THE COMING WORLD AND OUR HOPE

Having shared a few human expectations, goals, and hopes for a better world, we now turn to God's prophetic messages to answer *what the world is coming to.* Before answering this question, let's consider why we would want or need to know God's view. First, even though our human-planned ways of life seem good and right, God reminds us that there is a way that seems right to people, even spiritually-minded people, but the end of such a way leads to death (Proverbs 14:12; 16:25). The Bible reminds us that "it is better to take refuge in the Lord than to trust in man" (Psalm 118:8). Perhaps it says this because a strictly human way of life cannot always see its limitations and often fails to see the disruptive and deceitful evil nature in humans as an unfixable obstacle to reaching a sustainable, good world. God makes it clear that our trust in mankind instead of in God our Creator will not ultimately yield the positive results we hope for (Ecclesiastes 2:11-21; Jeremiah 17:5-11).

Second, we would want to know God's view of what the world is coming to because we live our daily lives in response to what is coming in the future. For example, I've planned a number of backpack trips to the mountains. I knew they were coming, so I prepared. I began jogging weeks ahead to get in shape for hiking and climbing. I gathered what was needed for the trip—a water purifier, tent, food, fishing gear, proper clothing, and so forth. Failure to do this could easily result in being caught off-guard and not having something I need for survival. Another example is college youth who study their lessons because they know a test is coming and do not want to fail. You get the point. It is valuable to know and understand what's coming if we are to know what we must do (1 Chronicles 12:32). God does not want us to be surprised by things that will take place but to be prepared. Paul said to believers, "The day of the Lord will come like a thief in the night . . . but you, brethren, are not in the darkness that the day would overtake you like a thief" (1 Thessalonians 5:2-4). How we prepare and get ready for what is coming depends on what we know is going to happen. Most people are clueless to what is coming, and they reject the warnings (Matthew 11:20-22).

Third, knowing God's view of the world's future is important because we humans know only what we have experienced or what others relate to us, and our observations and opinions may or may not be as correct or complete as they need to be. I like that there is a God who has given us information about the future of our world. It gives me a place to go where I can ascertain something that is more valid than my own thinking or understanding. We all need input from outside of ourselves that enables us to see things more clearly—not only from God but from each other. It is true that every one of us has something of value we can offer to others. We have learned much from human studies and life's experiences, but how valuable is learning from the God who knows infinitely more than we will ever know? God's truth and wisdom about many things is much needed, but unfortunately, his truth and wisdom are increasingly ignored resources (Proverbs 1:20-33). We miss needed, life-giving information if we ignore his warnings of what the world is coming to.

What does God say the world is coming to? It is said that history repeats itself—and it does, but not in endless cycles as some think. For according to the Bible, history is moving toward a final destination. It seems quite clear to Bible readers that the prophecies in the book of Daniel have to do with world history and where it is headed. These prophecies begin in chapter 2 with the king of Babylon, Nebuchadnezzar, who had a dream. The interpretation of the dream was given by God to Daniel to pass on to the king. God revealed that Nebuchadnezzar's dream was in reference to future world history (Daniel 2:27-29). The king's dreamt prophecy says there will be four kingdoms on earth leading up to a final forever-enduring kingdom established by God (Daniel 2:36-45).

Later, in chapter 7, Daniel records his own prophetic visions, the interpretation of which was made known to him. The dream was similar to the one in chapter 2 in that it also involved four world kingdoms followed by a kingdom of God. Daniel's vision reveals further information about the four kingdoms but especially the fourth kingdom. It is during this fourth kingdom that a king with great world influence will speak out against God and wear down God's saints, but God will judge him and destroy his rule, and his dominion will be given to the saints of God as an everlasting kingdom (Daniel 7:23-27).

In chapter 8 Daniel has another vision with further revelation about world kingdoms. The kingdom of the Medes and Persians is identified as the one following Nebuchadnezzar and Babylon. After the Medes and Persians, the kingdom of Greece is identified. World history tells us this kingdom was ruled by Alexander the Great and was subsequently divided out to four other rulers. As the book of Daniel continues, Daniel is given additional information about future world history, including a prophecy about the Jewish people and their Messiah (Daniel 9). Although prophetic detail of what happens in the very last days becomes more hidden, there is a prophecy about unparalleled distress from which God's people will be rescued (Daniel 12:1).

Daniel 12:4 mentions a future increase in knowledge, which has been interpreted in different ways. It says in the end of time, *knowledge will increase*. Has that time arrived? Some say, "Who would have thought we would see the explosion of readily available knowledge that we see today with our digital devices." Others interpret Daniel 12:4 as saying people will go all over trying to *increase their knowledge*, desiring to understand what's happening in the world, but will waste their efforts to find the truth because they are not searching in the right places. That is also true considering Daniel 12:10.

Finally, Daniel is told that God's words will be concealed and sealed up until the end, at which time further understanding will be given to those with insight (Daniel 12:9-10). The book closes with a promise to Daniel that he would rise and receive his "allotted portion at the end of the age" (Daniel 12:13).

In reading biblical prophecies, we discover that future government does have a part to play. Human leaders care about their world and are quite capable of perceiving threats to the well-being of the human race. After all, humankind does not want to see itself destroyed and will do all it can for self-preservation. Because of global problems such as violence, economic instability, and insurmountable human needs, it is likely that another of humanism's ideals, a worldwide governing body, will come into power as a fix-it-all. But as nations move toward a more global system of government, according to biblical prophecies, for some reason, a part of its leadership will eventually come to a place of open arrogance and defiance toward God, proclaiming human supremacy. This rebellion against God will include a heightened and hateful persecution of God's people, Christians and Jews alike. Such persecution has been repeated many times throughout history, but apparently, near the end of this present age, its severity will require God's intervention (Matthew 24:21-22; 2 Thessalonians 1:4-8).

Jesus told his disciples that because they would be hated by all nations, they could expect great tribulation from fellow humans. The world would hate them as it hated him because its people do not know God (Matthew 24:9; John 15:18-21). Concerning the Jews, it was prophesied that a day is coming in which nations will gather to battle against Jerusalem but that the Lord will go forth and fight against those nations (Zechariah 14:1-4). The Bible reminds us that all who desire to live godly lives in Christ Jesus should live in expectancy of persecution (2 Timothy 3:12). Not all will be persecuted to the same degree, and not all will be killed—some may be rescued and spared (Revelation 3:10-12; 6:9-11). We do not know how it all will unfold—God knows—but whatever happens, Christians are to trust God, be sustained by hope, and be faithful to Him.

Following are a number of prophecies telling of future leaders who defy God and promote the persecution of God's people. In Psalm 2 we learn about rulers of nations who take counsel together against the Lord and his Anointed (Psalm 2:1-3). This is a prophecy of rebellion toward God and his anointed Messiah, fulfilled in the days of Jesus. This view has the concurrence of the New Testament

(Acts 4:25-26).[6] Time will tell whether it will also apply to events beyond the days of Christ.

Referring again to Daniel, God revealed that a world leader is coming who will speak out against the Most High and wear down the saints of the Highest One (Daniel 7:13-27). Many have tried to identify persons and times in ancient history when these words were fulfilled, but even if this prophecy was partially fulfilled at earlier times, we can expect similar events to yet take place since the prophecy's inclusion of Christ's coming kingdom will take place during this fourth world kingdom, which is still future. The New Testament tells us that just before the next coming of the Lord Jesus, a man of lawlessness will be revealed who opposes and exalts himself above every so-called god and who displays himself as being God (2 Thessalonians 2:1-4).

One final prophecy worth mention is one given by Jesus to John the apostle and is about a ruler yet to arise who speaks arrogant words against God and who makes war with the saints (Revelation 13:3-8).

What can we make of these prophecies? I take the attitude of Daniel and the mother of Jesus, who, upon hearing God's words, treasured them and pondered them in mind and heart (Daniel 7:28; Luke 2:18-19, 51). Rather than dismiss them, I prefer to keep an expectant eye, waiting to see what will come. In light of these prophecies, as present history unfolds, I expect the supernatural God will continue to be denied and ignored in favor of the rise and power of mankind. The human race will continue with good-intentioned endeavors, living life as usual, thinking all is good. Global problems will likely pave the way for the welcoming acceptance of a government that offers world peace and safety, but in the end, accepted governing authorities will prove to be anti-God, cause great tribulation upon God's people (Revelation 7:9-14), and lead to God's final judgment upon the world.

If God's prophecies are true, what hope is there for obtaining a better world? God reveals that the world *will* come to an age of peace, unity, and total goodness, not under mankind's efforts but under the direction of Christ Jesus, who returns to earth, not in humble

---

6.   Note that this Old Testament prophetic psalm written by David is said to be from God's Holy Spirit.

servitude but as the world's Lord and King. Biblical prophecies tell us that Jesus will restore all things (Acts 3:17-21). When he comes, he will judge the world in righteousness and bring about the kind of evil-free world we long to experience (Acts 17:30-31). That Christ will be King and establish his kingdom to last forever is proclaimed throughout the Judean-Christian scriptures. In Psalm 2 God says he will install his King and give to him the nations as his inheritance. In Isaiah 9:6-7 God promises us a Son whose name is Mighty God and Prince of Peace, and there will be no end to the increase of his government. In Daniel 7:13-14 Daniel is given a vision of God's kingdom that will not be destroyed, where people from all nations will serve "One like a Son of Man." In Zechariah 14:4-9 God speaks of a coming day in which the Lord will stand on the Mount of Olives by Jerusalem and will be King over all the earth. In Luke 1:30-33 the mother of Jesus is told that her son will be great, and he will be given a throne, and his kingdom will have no end. In Revelation 19:11-16 we have an account of the coming of Jesus to strike down the nations and rule them as King of kings and Lord of lords. In Revelation 22:20 Jesus testifies, "I am coming quickly." *Amen. Come, Lord Jesus.*

Even though *in appearance* humans may seem to be achieving their objectives without God, can human-driven efforts guarantee that our world will reach its hoped-for state? According to the Bible, it is God who will establish a peaceful, loving, and war-free world (Isaiah 2:2-4).

OUR CHOICE BETWEEN TWO WORLDVIEWS

People in ancient Israel did not like to hear negative world-ending doom and judgment kinds of things but preferred and demanded messengers who only spoke good things. But they were not God's messages, only what the people wanted to hear (2 Chronicles 18:5-17; cp. 2 Timothy 4:1-4). And like King Herod of old, there continue to be many people who do not want Christ to rule over them, so they do not like to hear these things (Matthew 2:1-16). The idea that Jesus will one day return to earth to rule the world is mocked by many (2 Peter 3:3-4). No one has to believe these prophecies, and anyone can come up with reasons to discount them, but there they are, to this day, remaining in bold print for all to read.

For believers, what needs to be a Christ-honoring response? Do we as God's people abandon our fellow human beings and leave all to the fate of suffering the coming wrath and judgment of God (John 3:36)? God has not done so. He loves the world and still intends to redeem and save whosoever will believe in Christ Jesus (John 3:16). We must care as God cares, loving God and loving others, being lights of joy, justice, and hope in darkness (Matthew 5:14-16; 22:37-39; 1 Peter 2:9), demonstrating God's love and grace to a hurting world, continuing to do good alongside others who are working to overcome evil by doing the Lord's good.

I conclude with comments pointing out two primary differences between the humanistic worldview and God's views from the scriptures. First, it is obvious the two views have opposite directions of where the world is headed. Contrary to humanism's "*we* can make a good world," Jesus said that up to the end of this age, wars will exist (Matthew 24:6-7) and lawlessness will increase (Matthew 24:12). The Apostle Paul writes that in the last days, difficult times will come because of the evil and immoral nature within people. They will love themselves and their pleasures rather than God; they will be lovers of money, unloving, brutal, irreconcilable, without self-control, haters of good, unholy, and so forth (2 Timothy 3:1-5). But in human thinking, all is hopeful because they believe in the power of human goodness to overcome the negatives. In a humanistic world, people will continue living their daily lives as always—eating, drinking, marrying, buying and selling, pursuing their dreams, being religious, and thinking their world will arrive at peace and safety. But in God's view, they are without understanding of who God is and what the world is coming to (Proverbs 28:5; Matthew 24:37-39; Luke 17:26-30; 1 Thessalonians 5:2-3).

Second, the two views differ in the hope they have when it comes to their time to die. What is the hope of humans who live by humanistic ideals? The primary hope is that I can die happy with the knowledge that I have left the world a better place by loving my family and others, by having done good to help my fellow man, and by having helped influence the next generation to do the same. Also, I can die peacefully because I am now going to a better place—or going out of existence—whichever one's belief may be. But is all of that a guaranteed hope? It cannot be if this world is perishing—if in the end, evil and death wins (Ecclesiastes 2:18-23; 1 John 2:15-17). How does the Christian hope compare? Christians can die happy and peacefully knowing that, through faith in Christ Jesus, they have been loved, forgiven, and accepted by God. And as a result of their God-given life issuing forth in love for God and others, they can look forward to a new world that will be evil free and made up of loving relationships, meaningful social interaction, and gratifying activity. In the end, goodness and life wins.

Yes, according to biblical prophecies, Christian believers of a coming generation, who may be us, must be ready to suffer greater persecution (Romans 8:16-18). But as persons indwelt by Christ, nothing will be able to separate us from God's love and purpose for our lives (Zephaniah 3:14-20; Romans 8:31-39). If you are a sincere follower of Jesus, perhaps this chapter leaves you wondering how you will be able to live and survive in an increasingly hostile and non-Christian world. In the next chapter, we learn of the many kinds of persecutions Jesus faced, how he responded to those persecutions, and how he loved and lived in a culture with differing values from God's.

CHAPTER 3

JESUS' RESPONSES TO PERSECUTION AND SUFFERINGS

Peter, a disciple who was with Jesus throughout the years of his (Jesus') ministry and who eventually died for the cause of Christ, reports that Jesus was a man who "went about doing good" (Acts 10:38). When people brought to him those suffering with various diseases and pains, he healed them (Matthew 4:23-25; 8:17; 9:35). These healings fulfilled the prophet Isaiah's word: "He Himself took our infirmities and carried away our diseases" (Isaiah 53:4). Jesus was a man of compassion (Matthew 9:36; 14:14; 15:32; 20:34), healing the sick, feeding the hungry, proclaiming God's kingdom to the downcast, and forgiving the guilty. Large crowds followed him, and though he was loved and respected by many, Jesus was not oblivious to the world's evils and the corrupt nature within humankind. He knew that along the way, when people were confronted with his truth, he would incur their anger and persecution. The persecution Jesus suffered included being mocked, beaten, and nailed to a cross, all of which was unfair and unjust since he was innocent of all charges against him. Even Pilate, his Roman judge, believed him to be innocent and did not want to put him to death (Matthew 27:22-23; John 18:38; 19:4-6, 12).

If Jesus was a good man and innocent of all wrongdoing, why was he treated with rejection and contempt? Some, by noting his love and goodness in light of their lack of love and goodness, may have felt uneasy around him. Teachers and other leaders who had influence among the people, aware of his growing popularity, became jealous and fearful of being replaced—so much so that they plotted to kill him. Others were angered at him for speaking hard-to-swallow truth that pointed out their wrongs. Some who were invited to follow him were unwilling to give up what it would cost. Those who disagreed or misunderstood his teachings walked away, refusing to listen.

For a variety of reasons, he was rejected. He made people look at themselves. It seems very few honestly face who they are when the light of exposure draws near (John 3:19-20). But he did not come to judge them, nor did he condemn them; his love wanted to save them from their corrupt world (John 3:16-17). However, most did not perceive this; for in their minds, they did not need saving. Of course, there were those who were drawn to him and experienced his love and life-changing power. But his true followers soon discovered that the world would reject and persecute them as they did him. Jesus suffered much from an unbelieving world and promised the same to his followers (John 15:18-25). How would they handle their persecution? It would help them—and us—to see how Jesus responded to four kinds of persecution.

1: JESUS AND VERBAL ABUSE

First, we learn that Jesus suffered the persecution of *verbal abuse*. He had to endure his share of criticisms, name-calling, being made fun of, gossip, and false accusations. Some say verbal abuse is not suffering, but most of us know how words can hurt and destroy our well-being and valued relationships (Proverbs 18:21; James 3:8-9). I remember when a friend told me that a person in our community was spreading untruths about me that would ruin my reputation and cause people to think incorrectly of me. I contacted him as soon as possible before the damage had gone too far and resolved the issue. Thankfully, I never heard any more about it. Words can destroy. Following are a number of the verbal abuses Jesus suffered and had to endure.

He was criticized for being a *friend of sinners*, hanging out with the wrong crowd, being with bad people who he should avoid (Matthew 9:9-13). Jesus' response was, "It is not those who are healthy who need a physician, but those who are sick; I did not come to call the righteous, but sinners" (Mark 2:16-17). Once a week a pastor friend of mine went into one of the town bars. He did not enter into alcoholic drinking with the regulars or use the foul language some of them used, but he was with them, sipping coke, playing cards, and visiting with those who considered the bar their place of connecting. Here were people, like all of us, who enjoy being with others who accept them and with friends who listen as they vent their problems. My friend suffered criticism for going into a bar; after all, someone might see him, and he should be setting a good example by avoiding all appearance of evil. But after a time, some of those he befriended started coming to his church. Not all believers would feel called to do what he did, but can he be criticized in light of Jesus' response to *his* critics? Besides, why do believers think they are so different from anyone else? Are we not all sinners needing what Jesus offered, to be brought into God's kingdom of love and righteousness by the miraculous mercies of God?

Jesus was called a *blasphemer* for making himself out to be God (Matthew 26:65-66; Mark 2:7; 14:61-64; John 19:7). It was very sacrilegious (grossly irreverent) and offensive to God for a man to claim to be God or to be able to do what God alone can do (examples of this: Acts 12:21-23; 14:8-18). Naturally, they were wrong about Jesus' claims because he really was God who had come to earth in human flesh (Luke 1:30-35; John 1:1, 14). Jesus responded to their name-calling by answering that he *does* have the authority to say and do the things he does. Throughout his ministry years, the miracles he performed were evidences of the presence of the kingdom of God and of his divine authority, but his critics would not accept what these signs meant (Mark 2:8-12; John 2:18-22; 9:24-34). In our day, if I claimed to be equal with God, people would call me crazy, laugh, or ignore me. But what if I did the kinds of miracles Jesus did? Or rose from the dead? Jesus asked his disciples, "Who do people say that I am? Who do you say that I am?" (Mark 8:27-29).

Jesus was portrayed as a hypocrite for *breaking the Sabbath* (John 9:16). Keeping the Sabbath Day holy was one of the Ten Commandments and in Jewish culture is a very strict law of God (Exodus 20:8; Deuteronomy 5:12-15). Jesus was accused often of not living by this law, and people used it against him by saying that a person who disobeyed God could not be a true spokesman representing God (Matthew 12:9-14; Mark 2:23-28; Luke 13:10-16; John 5:10-18). Jesus did not break the Sabbath or disagree with God's law; rather, he corrected misunderstandings by saying, "the Sabbath was made for man, and not man for the Sabbath. So the Son of Man is Lord even of the Sabbath" (Mark 2:27-28). Rather than disobeying God's law, Jesus was doing the work of God the Father. So to condemn him for doing good on the Sabbath was to condemn the God they said they believed in (John 5:17). Likewise, when they condemned him for claiming to be equal with God, he said the same thing: "the Son does nothing of Himself, unless it is something He sees the Father doing" (John 5:18-20).

He goes on to tell them that if they do not honor him, they do not honor God the Father (John 5:23). He also says to them that if they do not believe in him, they will be subject to God's judgment and will not have eternal life (John 5:24). Later, he delivers a pretty harsh-sounding word to them when he tells them "they are unwilling to come to Him so that they may have life because they do not have the love of God in themselves" (John 5:40, 42). What if he said things like this to us? Would we believe what Jesus says and discover new life by listening to him, or would we be offended and too proud to believe the truth about ourselves and lose our life (Proverbs 13:13-14)?

Jesus was accused of being *possessed by the devil* (Matthew 9:32-34; 12:22-24; Mark 3:22). When he cast evil spirits out of people, some refused to believe that he was doing these works by the power of God but was performing them by the power of Satan. It is true that Satan has powers and *can* perform supernatural things to deceive people. Jesus did warn us not to be misled by false messages from persons able to perform supernatural powers (Matthew 24:24). We must discern whether or not a spirit is from God (1 John 4:1). I once visited a person who communicated with spirits through spirit writing. He claimed these spirits were from God and were helping him. When I asked him to tell me more about his experience, he told me that as long as he continued to commit more and more of his life to these spirits, they would continue to guide him (consider 2 Corinthians 11:14). When I challenged him by saying these were not God's spirits, he sat down at a table and, after a few moments of writing, said the spirits told him not to listen to me. I felt I was in a battle for his soul and would not leave until he made a decision about who he would follow: these spirits or the Spirit of Christ. His decision was to stay with these spirits because they were giving him what Jesus would not: clear guidance for his life. I tell this story to indicate that in our day, evil spirits still have people under their influence and in bondage.[7] When Jesus was accused of casting out spirits by the power of Satan, his response was to give his critics a lesson in logic on how a kingdom divided against itself cannot stand, and that, on the contrary, his power of casting out demons was an act of God that demonstrated that the kingdom of God had come upon them (Matthew 12:25-30).

Those who hated Jesus and wanted to prove him a false prophet would send people to *test him with a question*. They hoped Jesus would answer the question wrongly so they could publicly discredit him as a teacher or find some accusation that would get him in trouble with the religious establishment or Roman government (Matthew 22:15-22). Jesus perceived their trickery and was able to answer wisely and keep from incriminating himself.

Jesus was falsely accused of being a *troublemaker* and a *traitor* who stirred up the people to riot and who was creating rebellion against the Roman government (Luke 23:1-2, 5, 13-14; John 19:12). When he was examined on these charges, Pilate, with authority to judge on behalf of the Roman government, found no proof of these accusations and declared that Jesus was innocent of the charges. But Jesus' accusers persisted, and eventually Pilate gave in to their demands and condemned him to be crucified (John 19:13-16). During all of

7. God warned people to avoid supernatural contacts with spiritists, mediums, spell casters, witches, fortune-tellers, and so forth, for God knows what trouble we can get into (Deuteronomy 18:9-14). But people are drawn to such powers, aren't they?

this, Jesus witnessed to Pilate about who he was (John 18:33-37). Jesus also said some things to answer his accusers (John 18:19-23). But overall, when accusations and charges were brought against him, Jesus did not seek to gain his freedom by defending himself (Matthew 26:62-63; 27:12-14). Jesus knew that God's will for him was to die for the sins of all people that they might be reconciled to God and receive eternal life through repentance and faith (Isaiah 53; Mark 1:14-15; John 3:16). No one could take his life; he voluntarily gave up his life for all of us (John 10:17-18).[8]

To summarize observations about Jesus' handling of people's verbal abuses, we can say that mostly he would correct their comments by countering with the truth. Apparently it is OK *not to allow* people to believe what they want but to let them know how things really are. I sometimes kid my three-year-old grandson by giving him a name that is not his real name, and he tells me, "No," and he corrects me by telling me his real name and what he wants to be called. Is that the approach we need to take with people who criticize us or call us names? I have heard Christians criticized or accused of things like, "You think you are better than us," or, "The church is full of hypocrites." If someone said this to you or me, what would we answer to correct their thinking? Sometimes Jesus did not answer his critics because he saw it would do no good, and they would not accept it anyway. But if that was the case, he would tell them so (Luke 22:67). On the other hand, when people criticize or call *us* names, we may need to consider what they say as possibly being true about us. Through our critics, God may be trying to help us correct something that needs to be changed in our Christian walk (Proverbs 15:32-33; 2 Samuel 16:5-11). If that is so, agreeing with them needs to be included in an honest answer, along with the truth

---

8. Isaiah prophesied that this suffering servant of God would not open his mouth (Isaiah 53:7). The following comment was written by Eric Lyons in an article published by *Apologetics Press*: "To prophesy that the 'Suffering Servant opened not His mouth,' is to use a Hebrew idiom and hyperbolic expression which means that Jesus refrained from giving an exhaustive legal defense on His own behalf. During much of His affliction and oppression He was completely silent (cf. Matthew 26:62-63; 27:12-14). At other times He spoke only a few words—none of which comes close to being the kind of defense He could have offered on His own behalf had He been trying to avoid persecution and crucifixion." (www.apologeticspress.org.).

of what they are not seeing. Overall, I would think that we need to avoid defending ourselves and simply tell people God's truth about the matters they bring up. Most of the time, Jesus respectfully and calmly answered those who verbally persecuted him.

2: JESUS IS UNACCEPTED BY HIS COMMUNITY AND FAMILY

A second form of persecution Jesus suffered was being *marginalized*; that is, he was rejected and ostracized by his community (Isaiah 53:3). He was *rejected by the religious establishment* when they tried to have him arrested to keep him from spreading his teachings (John 7:32, 45-52). There was a division among the common people concerning him (John 7:12, 25, 40-44), undoubtedly caused by the differing opinions of their religious leaders over who Jesus was. Perhaps, knowing their leaders opposed Jesus, they were confused about what to think, but whatever the reason, this division kept many from accepting him.

Jesus regularly attended synagogue meetings. In one synagogue he was welcomed to come to the front, read from the scriptures, and comment on what he read. It didn't help his favor with the people when what he said so angered them that they got up and threw him out of the synagogue, driving him out of the city to the edge of a cliff. They would have cast him over had he not escaped (Luke 4:28-30). On another occasion, many who had been following him did not like a particular teaching, so they stopped being his supporters and left him (John 6:66). Certainly it did not help Jesus' image when he used a whip to drive merchants out of the temple area (John 2:13-21). Rumors were that Jesus wanted to destroy their temple. People talk, and word gets around. I suppose it was the sum of a number of these happenings that created divisions among the people about who he was.

Some *people thought he was insane*. Even Jesus' family, when they heard a disturbing report about him, believed he was crazy and had *lost his senses*. So they went to get him and bring him home, but he would not have it (Mark 3:20-21; John 10:20). His comment about family was, "Who are My mother and My brothers? Whoever does the will of God, he is My brother and sister and mother" (Mark 3:31-35). Were statements like this a cause of alienating even more listeners? As popular as Jesus was, he certainly had his critics and enemies. During the trial that led to his death, Jesus was mockingly dressed as a king; they placed a crown on his head and put a robe on him and bowed down before him, making fun of him and spitting on him. To them, he was a big joke (Matthew 27:27-31).

Perhaps Christ's most horrible rejection came from God the Father, who would not remove his sufferings and agony of death on the cross. We get a sense he must have felt the emotional pain of *abandonment* when he cried out from the cross, "My God, My God, why have you forsaken Me" (Psalm 22:1-2, 11, 16; Matthew 27:46). Many people have been rejected, abandoned, disappointed, or betrayed by someone they loved. They understand how devastating these feelings can be. How did Jesus handle such rejections? With some like Judas, who meant to do evil, he used a question to make them conscious of what they were doing: "Judas, are you betraying the Son of Man with a kiss?" (Luke 22:47-48). With some like Peter, who gave way to his fears, Jesus prayed for restoration and later gave reassurance of his continued love and forgiveness (Luke 22:31-34, 55-61; John 21:15-19).

3–4: Jesus Handles Physical Persecution and Death

Third, Jesus suffered *physical aspects of persecution.* This mostly happened during the trial preceding his crucifixion. He had escaped physical abuse earlier, but during his trial he suffered being spit upon, being blindfolded and beaten with fists, being slapped, having a crown of thorns shoved down on his head, and being brutally whipped, leaving him very weak and with a body full of ripped-open flesh and bleeding wounds (Mark 14:53-65; 15:15-20; John 19:1-3).

How did Jesus respond to these ill-mannered, disrespectful, irreverent, degrading, and punishing treatments? As an example for us, he suffered them without resistance, revenge, or threats, and he entrusted his life to God who would make things right in the end (1 Peter 2:20-23). Having overcome his human struggles and mental anguish through a prayer time with the Father, he accepted God's will for him as was prophesied in scripture—to suffer and die in order to bring us a new life and peace with God, self, and others (Isaiah 50:6; 53; Matthew 16:21; Colossians 1:19-22).

Fourth, Jesus suffered a tortuous *death through execution* on a Roman cross. Crucifixion was an extreme and painful punishment administered to criminals. On a hill for all to see, they removed his outer clothing, exposing him to public ridicule and shame, and by driving nails through his hands (or wrists) and feet, they fastened him to a wooden cross (Luke 23:33; 24:39-40; John 19:23-24). After about six hours of hanging on the cross (Mark 15:25; Luke 23:44), he gave up his life with the words, "It is finished," and, "Father, into your hands I commit my spirit" (Luke 23:46; John 19:30).

How did Jesus respond to those who treated him so cruelly and unjustly? He said, "Father, forgive them; for they do not know what they are doing" (Luke 23:34). The great good news is that, in spite of Jesus' persecutors putting him to death, it was not the end of his life. His dead body was resurrected, and he lives forever. Bodily resurrection is the certain hope of all who believe in Jesus and have been given the gift of his Spirit (John 11:25-26; Romans 8:9-11). No wonder Jesus could say, "Do not fear those who kill the body" (Matthew 10:28). Interestingly, although Jesus felt abandoned by his Father (Matthew 27:46), in the end he was able to say with all confidence, "Father, into your hands I commit My spirit" (Luke 23:46). His hope was paradise, not death. So it is with all who trust God and his word of hope (Acts 7:54-60).

JESUS' TEACHINGS ABOUT PERSECUTION

What did Jesus teach about responding to those who persecute or mistreat us? Following are a number of his teachings that could possibly be applied to situations in which we find ourselves. When surveying these teachings, we must keep in mind that not all apply to every situation. The context of our lives in any given moment determines which teachings apply. If we are not currently going through persecution, these words of Jesus will probably not have a present impact on our lives. The best time to read or remember them will be when we are suffering at the hands of others. During such times, these teachings will most certainly contribute much to helping us.

The big question is, *Can I do what he says?* It is not easy to practice Jesus' teachings. For example, Jesus said not to fear in the face of death, but fear is a common protective response in humans, and it can be very difficult *not* to fear (just ask Peter). We shall briefly address how to deal with fear after we review the following teachings of Jesus as quoted from the scriptures.

Blessed are those who have been persecuted for the sake of righteousness, for theirs is the kingdom of heaven. Blessed are you when people insult you and persecute you, and falsely say all kinds of evil against you because of Me. Rejoice and be glad, for your reward in heaven is great; for in the same way they persecuted the prophets who were before you. (Matthew 5:10-12)

You have heard that it was said, "AN EYE FOR AN EYE, AND A TOOTH FOR A TOOTH." But I say to you, do not resist an evil person; but whoever slaps you on your right cheek, turn the other to him also. If anyone wants to sue you and take your shirt, let him have your coat also. Whoever forces you to go one mile, go with him two. Give to him who asks of you, and do not turn away from him who wants to borrow from you. You have heard that it was said, "YOU SHALL LOVE YOUR NEIGHBOR and hate your enemy." But I say to you, love your enemies and pray for those who persecute you, so that you may be sons of your Father who is in heaven; for He causes His sun to rise on the evil and the good, and sends rain on the righteous and the unrighteous. For if you love those who love you, what reward do you have? Do not even the tax collectors do the same? If you greet only your brothers, what more are you doing than others? Do not even the Gentiles do the same? Therefore you are to be perfect, as your heavenly Father is perfect. (Matthew 5:38-48)

If you forgive others for their transgressions, your heavenly Father will also forgive you. But if you do not forgive others, then your Father will not forgive your transgressions. (Matthew 6:14-15)

Behold, I send you out as sheep in the midst of wolves; so be shrewd as serpents and innocent as doves. But beware of men, for they will hand you over to the courts and scourge you in their synagogues; and you will even be brought before governors and kings for My sake, as a testimony to them and to the Gentiles. But when they hand you over, do not worry about how or what you are to say; for it will be given you in that hour what you are to say. For it is not you who speak, but it is the Spirit of your Father who speaks in you. Brother will betray brother to death, and a father his child; and children will rise up against parents and cause them to be put to death. You will be hated by all because of My name, but it is the one who has endured to the end who will be saved. But whenever they persecute you in one city, flee to the next; for truly I say to you, you will not finish going through the cities of Israel until the Son of Man comes. (Matthew 10:16-23)

In a similar way these are the ones on whom seed was sown on the rocky places, who, when they hear the word, immediately receive it with joy; and they have no firm root in themselves, but are only temporary; then, when affliction or persecution arises because of the word, immediately they fall away. (Mark 4:16-17)

And He summoned the crowd with His disciples, and said to them, "If anyone wishes to come after Me, he must deny himself, and take up his cross and follow Me. For whoever wishes to save his life will lose it, but whoever loses his life for My sake and the gospel's will save it. For what does it profit a man to gain the whole world, and forfeit his soul? For what will a man give in exchange for his soul? For whoever is ashamed of Me and My words in this adulterous and sinful generation, the Son of Man will also be ashamed of him when He comes in the glory of His Father with the holy angels." (Mark 8:34-38)

I say to you, My friends, do not be afraid of those who kill the body and after that have no more that they can do. But I will warn you whom to fear: fear the One who, after He has killed, has authority to cast into hell; yes, I tell you, fear Him! Are not five sparrows sold for two cents? Yet not one of them is forgotten before God. Indeed, the very hairs of your head are all numbered. Do not fear; you are more valuable than many sparrows. (Luke 12:4-7)

But before all these things, they will lay their hands on you and will persecute you, delivering you to the synagogues and prisons, bringing you before kings and governors for My name's sake. It will lead to an opportunity for your testimony. So make up your minds not to prepare beforehand to defend yourselves; for I will give you utterance and wisdom which none of your opponents will be able to resist or refute. But you will be betrayed even by parents and brothers and relatives and friends, and they will put some of you to death, and you will be hated by all because of My name. Yet not a hair of your head will perish. By your endurance you will gain your lives. (Luke 21:12-19)

Be on guard, so that your hearts will not be weighted down with dissipation and drunkenness and the worries of life, and that day will not come on you suddenly like a trap; for it will come upon all those who dwell on the face of all the earth. But keep on the alert at all times, praying that you may have strength to escape all these things that are about to take place, and to stand before the Son of Man. (Luke 21:34-36)

"These things I have spoken to you, so that in Me you may have peace. In the world you have tribulation, but take courage; I have overcome the world." (John 16:33)

When they came to the place called the Skull, there they crucified Him and the criminals, one on the right and the other on the left. But Jesus was saying, "Father forgive them; for they do not know what they are doing." And they cast lots, dividing His garments among themselves. (Luke 23:33-34; see also Psalm 22:18)

The Importance of Prayer in Times of Persecution

We do not know what we will have to endure in the future, but anger or fears can overtake us. Jesus helps prepare us for such times. Just before Jesus' arrest and the coming persecution of his disciples, Jesus led them to a place of prayer (Matthew 26:31-39). Having intimate communion with God is essential for successfully facing fearful and difficult times. Jesus' disciples learned the importance of prayer, even in their failure to pray. Jesus said to them, "You could not watch with me for one hour? Keep watching and praying that you may not enter into temptation; the spirit is willing, but the flesh is weak" (Matthew 26:40-41). Temptations can lead us to become despondent or fearful rather than courageous, triumphant, and hope-filled. We cannot face persecution on our own but must rely on the grace of God. Amidst the Apostle Paul's sufferings and persecutions, he was reminded by the Lord, "My grace is sufficient for you, for power is perfected in weakness" (2 Corinthians 12:9-10). Grace can be defined as God's power or enablement given by him to help us. We ask for it because, on our own, we know we cannot do what needs doing, nor can we give ourselves the peace of mind we long for. As Jesus did in Gethsemane, the help we need comes when we totally surrender our lives and situation to God, knowing that without what he can give us, we are subject to defeat. We surrender through honest humility, confessing our struggles, our worries, and our fears, and we resist unbelief and trust God to give us what we need (1 John 4:4).

In prayer we also commit ourselves afresh to serving God's will for his glory and not ours (Psalm 115:1). Often times it is not that we don't know what to do but that we are unwilling to do it. We must ask God to glorify himself through us and resolve that whatever his will is for us, we will accept it and do it. During times of affliction, we need his guidance. We need to know whether he would have us stay engaged or flee a situation. We need the right words to say (Proverbs 15:28) or to know if silence is more appropriate (Proverbs 17:27-28; 21:23). We need him to give us the proper attitude in addressing persons with whom we are involved, whether they are for us or against us. Instead of leaving everything up to God, thinking that God will do it all for us, it is important to say to him, "God, what would you have me do?" Listening for his answer is another difficult task, but we have the printed Word of God as a place to begin. God also would have us rely on our fellow believers for supporting counsel and encouragement (Proverbs 11:14; 24:5-6; Hebrews 3:12-14).

When overcome by inner turmoil and trials, prayer becomes a fortress, a place of safety where we retreat and hide until we recover our strength to re-enter the battle. "The name of the Lord is a strong tower, the righteous runs into it and is safe" (Proverbs 18:10). Like Jesus, we need to seek a solitary place to spend time with the Lord. Even if we cannot get away to a physical place, we can internally enter our place of safety and be renewed by drawing near to God and having him draw near to us (2 Chronicles 15:2; James 4:8). In that place, we do two things: first we cast our anxieties on him, trusting and knowing that he cares for us (1 Peter 5:7), and second, we take the time to focus on the love he has for us and the hope he gives us (Hebrews 7:18-19; 1 John 4:16). To feel within ourselves the love God has for us gives us a sense of safety and joy and a peace that everything will be all right (John 14:27; 16:33). The power of what experiencing God's love can do for us in a moment of need is amazing (Romans 8:34-39).

Focusing on our hope has a very key role in helping us overcome our sufferings. Precious knowledge of our guaranteed future can give us joy and peace in the midst of sufferings. As the Bible says, "The sufferings of this present time are not worthy to be compared to the glory that is to be revealed to us" (Romans 8:18; consider also 1 Corinthians 2:9).

I could not close this chapter in any better way than to have you read Psalm 91. I think Jesus would speak those words of wisdom and comfort to give us courage and strength to face life as he did. In fact, as we read them and let them sink in, he is speaking to us.

CHAPTER 4

BEING GOOD NEWS IN A BAD NEWS WORLD

We live in troublesome times. I hear many people complain about all the bad news they hear or read about, especially on TV and in the newspapers. Bad news is a common occurrence in a world like ours.

Some of that bad news involves Christians. I recently came across another story of adversity Christians face in other parts of the world. The home of a Christian family was entered and family members killed or wounded. The remaining family ran and hid nearby where they could hear the ravaging sounds of their house being ransacked and possessions stolen. Fearing to return home, they fled to a place of safety, grief-stricken over their horrific losses. Perhaps you think that kind of Christian persecution will never happen in our country. Maybe not, but there has long been an attitude of *no worries* by Christians who have enjoyed their country's freedom of religion, while in other countries, Christians, at the risk of imprisonment or fines, are not even allowed to speak their faith in public.

Be comforted that not everyone in the world is suffering at the hands of others; most may never experience it, but nevertheless, many are sensing that in our *thought-to-be-civilized* world, Christians are living in increasingly troublesome, even perilous times. Of course, from the first century on, I suppose nearly every generation of Christians had similar thoughts about their own times (Acts 8:1-3; Revelation 2:10). My focus in this chapter is to share stories from the Bible to learn how others have responded to difficult days. My prayer is that the Lord will give you and me a few insights from these stories in how to live and survive in troublesome days and be good news in a bad news world.

GODLY RESPONSES OF FAITH AND HOPE AMIDST ADVERSITY

In the last chapter we learned that Jesus' sufferings at the hands of others was something he promised would also happen to his lifelong committed followers (John 15:20). Christian persecution exists when a society's people become antagonistic toward believers and inflict various degrees of pain and suffering upon them. The Apostle Peter says that if we become believers and our lives are changed, if we no longer live for self-gratification but for the will of God, we will suffer rejection and be maligned because we no longer do the things with friends we used to do—things like sensuous and lustful activities and drinking parties (1 Peter 4:1-4).

According to the Bible, there are right reasons and wrong reasons for being persecuted. There are also right responses and wrong responses. We do not want to be persecuted because we are being hypocrites, living worldly lifestyles rather than obeying Jesus' teachings, or for being self-righteous and judgmental. Peter instructs us that if we are persecuted, it is to be for doing right and not wrong (1 Peter 2:12; 3:16-17). Taking a stand for right invites persecution. But if we keep a clear conscience by doing right, maintaining pure motives, and suffering for righteousness' sake, we need not fear intimidation or be troubled by others' abusive actions toward us (1 Peter 3:13-14).

Peter reminds us of responses Jesus would have us make. We are not to revile, call them names, or get even with them but are to entrust our life to God's justice—that he will repay those who are against us (1 Peter 2:21-23). Such responses free us to pray for others, to be concerned for their welfare, and to perform acts of kindness toward them (Matthew 5:44).

Furthermore, if we do suffer for our faith, we do not want to see ourselves as pitiful unjustly-treated victims. Rather, we are persons considered worthy to share in the sufferings of Jesus (Matthew 5:12; Acts 5:41; Philippians 3:10-11). Suffering is an opportunity to practice faith and hope toward God and to share our hope with those who have none (1 Peter 3:15).

Unfortunately, Christians are not the only ones to suffer injustice at the hands of others. Many minority peoples can also be the subjects of abuses. As we compassionately identify with any who are downtrodden, we may have opportunity to help them by bringing relief and justice (Galatians 6:9-10). For example, Christians in certain cities of the world are helping girls to get out of their slavery in sex trafficking by getting the guilty traffickers to court, by providing the victimized girls with a safe place to live, by teaching the girls skills so they can make a respectable living, and by offering counsel to help the victims overcome emotional trauma. Another example of helping the downtrodden would be to support and speak up for minorities who are being teased and harassed in your presence.

Those who have seen modern-day reality shows on their media screens have witnessed people being placed in the midst of adverse conditions with the goal of having to learn how to survive. In the chapter "What's the World Coming To? What Is Our Hope?" we were reminded of biblical prophecies telling us we can expect the world to become more widely anti-Christian and anti-Israel as the time for Christ's return to earth draws nearer (Daniel 7:19-27; Zechariah 14:2-4; Matthew 24:3, 9-10, 21-22). Living in a world that is becoming more and more antagonistic toward God and his people—a world that threatens persecution—can easily bring about the question, *How am I to live and survive in the midst of it?* Many of us who have thankfully enjoyed lives of relative ease must now consider the reality that our ease may not last. Three brief thoughts are encouraging: First, fear can be overcome through experiencing God's love and trusting his hope (Proverbs 29:25; 1 John 4:18). Second, there are those who respect believers for their faith and who may desire Jesus in their lives; we need to be there for them (Acts 17:32-34). Third, God strengthens and matures his people through adverse conditions (Psalm 119:67, 71).

Leaving you to ponder those thoughts, let's review a few life stories from the Bible that are examples of life-giving hope in the midst of adversity. They demonstrate how people can be good news and givers of hope among those who do not believe in the same God they do.

Attitudes and Deeds of Persons Suffering Adversity or Persecution

Jeremiah, a prophet of God in Israel, went through extreme times of affliction when God used an enemy nation to judge his people for their sins and destroy their cities and nation (Jeremiah 32:26-35). Before Israel fell, Jeremiah was nearly killed by his own people because they did not like his message of God's coming judgment (Jeremiah 38:4-6). Seeing his people killed, his nation overrun, his city destroyed, and many taken captive to a foreign land, Jeremiah suffered intense emotional pain, for he was part of them. What did he do? Where did he find peace? How did he survive such cruel times? Here are four things he did.

1. He honestly cried out to God his complaints and the pain he was feeling (Lamentations 2:11; 3:1-8, 17-18, 52-56).

2. Even though he was a godly man, he accepted and admitted he deserved God's judgment, the same as everyone else, for he too was a sinner (Lamentations 1:20-22; 3:39-40).

3. He remembered and believed God is compassionate, gracious, and good (Lamentations 3:21-25).

4. In the midst of ongoing afflictions, he exercised his faith and hope in God, and the result for him was that his life was spared (Jeremiah 15:10-21; 39:11-12; Lamentations 3:24, 57-58).

Will we who trust God experience similar results and escape from our afflictions? Maybe yes, maybe no. We are encouraged to have the attitude and spirit of three men who were taken captive in Israel's downfall. Jeremiah could have known them. They were now living in a foreign culture among worshippers of false gods. One day they were about to be killed for obeying their faith and standing against what they knew was wrong. When asked if their God would save them, they responded, "Our God whom we serve is able to deliver us . . . and He will deliver us. . . . But even if He does not . . . we are not going to serve your gods" (Daniel 3:17-18). It is also good to take on the attitude of the Apostle Paul when he was being persecuted for his faith (1 Corinthians 4:11-13). He said, "We had the sentence of death within ourselves so that we would not trust in ourselves, but in God who raises the dead" (2 Corinthians 1:8-9).

"But," you may say, "I am not like those great men of God, men of strong faith. I am only a common person and see little reason God should favor and rescue me." God favors the rich or poor, known or unknown. When Jeremiah's enemies threw him into a pit in order to put him to death, a person we rarely hear about helped him escape (Jeremiah 38:7-13). Have you heard of Ebed-melech the Ethiopian? Not likely. Here was a man who could easily go unnoticed, but God noticed the good thing he did, sent him a word of hope, and rescued him from future harm (Jeremiah 39:15-18). Even the least of us can do good deeds and be good news in the midst of wickedness. Ebed did as God says: "Do not be overcome by evil, but overcome evil with good (Romans 12:21).

One of my favorite Bible stories about common ordinary people surviving in troublesome times occurs in the days of Elijah, a prophet God worked through to do amazing miracles. To me, the story is not so much about Elijah as it is about a poor widow lady and her young son who struggled to survive a severe famine. When Elijah met her, she was near the gate of a city, gathering a few pieces of wood. Elijah asked her to bring him some bread. Her words have been recorded: "I have no bread, only a handful of flour in a bowl and a little oil in a jar, and I am gathering sticks that I may go in and prepare for me and my son, that we may eat and die" (1 Kings 17:8-12).

There are things about her in the story that convince me she must have had the fears and worrisome concerns we all might have in her situation, but what amazes me about her story is her seemingly peaceful state of mind in accepting her own and her family's death. But God saw her and knew her plight. Instead of suffering death, God provided for her needs by sending Elijah to her. She was a common, ordinary woman, lost from sight in a vast sea of uncaring faces—but God sees and cares about all of us (1 Peter 5:7). Do you believe this, and will it comfort you even in a time of imminent death? If we are going to survive dire times in our lives, we must be prepared to die. Knowing we are loved by God, trusting his love, and knowing our hope is a big part of that preparation.

LIVING UNDER GOVERNMENTS THAT ARE UNFAVORABLE TOWARD CHRISTIANS

How do hope-filled Christians live under governments not in sympathy with their beliefs? The Apostle Paul lived at a time when his governing authorities, whether Roman or Jewish, were not favorable toward Christians. There were times in Roman history, as in some countries today, when people were treated as criminals or traitors for being Christian. Paul suffered much persecution, was imprisoned a number of times, and eventually, according to tradition, was beheaded during the reign of the Roman emperor, Nero. Even if we cannot say with absolute certainty when or how he died, from a letter he wrote to a fellow worker named Timothy, we do know that he was aware of the nearness of his death (2 Timothy 4:6-8). In the letter, it is instructive to note Paul's hope in the face of death. It is also instructive, in light of living under anti-Christian governing authorities, to read what Paul said on the subject of government. Though some may find themselves in disagreement with what Paul taught, he did not say to fight against the government or put it down; he said we are to respect and be in subjection to the governing authorities, for their authority is established by God. Paul wrote, "Therefore, whoever resists authority has opposed the ordinance of God; and they who have opposed will receive condemnation upon themselves. . . . It is a minister of God to you for good. . . . For because of this you also pay taxes . . ." (Romans 13:1-7; see also Matthew 17:24-27). Wow! We certainly have to wonder how some governments could be God's instruments for good. In some situations with governing authorities, we will find ourselves having to do as Jesus said: "Love your enemies, and pray for those who persecute you" (Matthew 5:44).

Based on God's Word, we need to respect and obey the aims and laws of our governing authorities. However, the early apostles made it clear there are times when, if asked to do something clearly against the instructions of God, we are to obey God rather than man's authority (Acts 5:27-32). This does not mean to become destructive or violent as a way to object or resist. Applying the Apostle Peter's reminder, if we are persecuted by anyone, it should not be due to our misbehavior or any wrongdoing or because of acts of rebellion, but our suffering should be on account of following the lifestyle and directions of our Lord Jesus. If we must suffer punishment for our disobedience, so be it. We accept it as sharing the sufferings of our Lord. Also, if we do have the opportunity to appeal our case or to speak God's truth about an issue to governing authorities (whether policemen, mayors, governors, judges, presidents, kings, or their representatives), we should do so with gentleness and reverence (1 Peter 3:13-17). Wisdom reminds us that a gentle answer turns away wrath and a soothing tongue is a tree of life (Proverbs 15:1, 4). Tremper Longman III, in his book on Proverbs, reminds us that a wise person normally uses gentle words, though on occasion, strong words may be necessary.[9]

WORKING ALONGSIDE THOSE NOT SHARING OUR GODLY CONVICTIONS

In the book of Genesis, the story is told of Joseph who as a teenager was hated by his brothers and sold into a life of slavery in Egypt. There he lived as a servant in a nation of people that did not know his God. As he worked in what we would call secular jobs, he faithfully respected and diligently served his boss's wishes while at the same time being faithful to God and resisting temptations to live in the sins of the world.

One day he was falsely accused of an immoral act and was unjustly sentenced to prison, where he remained for over two years. Even in prison he lived in such a godly way in his speech, honesty, and hard work that those in authority respected and favored him, and he became a trusted servant of the head jailor. As the Bible states,

9. Tremper Longman III, *How to Read Proverbs* (Downers Grove, IL: InterVarsity Press Academic, 2002), 152.

oftentimes "when a man's ways are pleasing to the Lord, He makes even his enemies to be at peace with him" (Proverbs 16:7). Eventually, through God-directed circumstances, Joseph was released from prison and given the opportunity to serve those in higher governing positions. Though they did not believe in his God, Joseph demonstrated respect for the authorities he was under, did his assigned work to the best of his ability, and exhibited a desire to bless those over him by considering their goals and doing the right things to promote their profit and well-being. Again, he did all of this without entering into the sins of the people; he lived an exemplary godly life.

Even in his painful and unjust experiences, Joseph faithfully served his God, and God blessed his life so that those over him liked him. Can non-Christian people respect and like Christians? Not all will, but it certainly helps God's cause if they do. (You can follow Joseph's life story in Genesis 37, 39–41.)

Daniel was another believer in God who was forced to live among people and under a government that did not believe in God. He was taken captive, brought into their country, and being considered a youth with potential he was chosen to be educated in the language and customs of the people so that he could serve in the king's realm. From Daniel, we learn some of the things he did to blossom in an environment that was ignorant of his God and thus be God's good news in a bad news world. We notice that Daniel began with a personal decision. He believed God had standards, and he chose to follow God's standards—no matter what. One of those standards was to avoid foods God had forbidden him. Although the specific will of God we are to obey may differ from Daniel's, we are all called to decide if we will faithfully follow God's will or our own—or compromise. Daniel was firm in his decision not to defile himself with things prohibited by God (Daniel 1:5-8). This is where right living begins for all of us: determining not to defile ourselves by living in disobedience to God's Word.

How did Daniel handle his situation when told to do something he knew would displease God? He appealed to the authority over him by politely asking permission to not eat the food they wanted him to eat, and he explained the reason why. He relied on God for the right attitude, well thought-through wording, and a godly way of presenting himself. God gave Daniel wisdom, favor, and compassion in the sight of his superior.

When Daniel's overseer told him that for various reasons he could not change things, Daniel listened, took those reasons into consideration, and made a counterproposal that would satisfy the concerns of all involved. A wise saying in the Bible tells us that the heart of the righteous ponders how to answer and that there are times when sweetness of speech increases persuasiveness (Proverbs 15:28; 16:21). The overseer saw the reasonableness of Daniel's proposal, saw that it would not put him at risk with his superiors, and was willing to try it. Since his purpose was to please and obey God, Daniel prayed and trusted that God would honor his proposal and cause all to work for good, which it did (Daniel 1:9-16; Romans 8:28).

As this story shows, even if others do not believe in your God, many will respect and like you as a person if you present yourself in a genuinely compassionate, respectful, and kind way, showing concern for the other's well-being. Daniel then proceeded to be the best student he could be, learning everything the Babylonians wanted him to learn about their ways and customs and beliefs. In the end, he proved to be a gifted student, and by God's gifts and grace working in his life, Daniel was accepted into the king's service (Daniel 1:17-21). When future problems arose, even involving kings, Daniel used this same listening/discerning/reasoning, concern-for-others approach. He always asked God's help to work out any given situation and gave God thanks when he did (Daniel 2:12-23). If God wants to accomplish something through you to bring his love and message of salvation and hope to others, he will give you skills, grace, and wisdom to make it happen.

Over time, people observed and knew that Daniel was committed to his God. As you follow the life of Daniel, you will see that he lived for seventy or more years in a good relationship with numerous governing authorities, and when given appropriate opportunities, he was able to tell them and others about the God who was so powerfully exhibited in and through his life (Daniel 2:27-28, 47; 5:18-23). Only God knows how many may have come to know the Lord through his exemplary life and witness.

Daniel's life was not without persecution. One day, persons jealous of him and his position determined to find a way to have him killed. They came to the king with an evil-intentioned proposal. The king listened to them but did not see their wicked intentions. The commanded law throughout the kingdom was that anyone putting any god or other person above the king would be killed. What did Daniel do? He found out what had happened, went home, and as was his daily practice, he prayed to God in plain view of others. I wonder if Daniel, from the beginning, made a life plan of something he could visibly and continuously do to show others the source of his godly beliefs and lifestyle. For example, I knew a man who could not hear very well, but he came to church every week. When I asked why he came if he could not hear and understand what was being said, he told me he comes just to show people whose side he is on. When Daniel's enemies saw him openly praying to God, they accused him to the king. Reminding the king of the law he signed, they urged that Daniel be killed. Even though the king's heart grieved for Daniel, who he liked very much, he had to keep the law and ordered Daniel to be executed by being thrown to lions.

Throughout his life, we see how Daniel stays true to God, even if it costs him his life. We see that Daniel had a reputation of faithfully living for God. We see his absolute trust that God was at work in and through his life. We see that in all his jobs, he did the best work he could do to get the job done. We see his love for the people around him and his desire to serve and meet their needs. In the end, God spared Daniel's life from hungry lions, and the king was so impressed with Daniel's God that he made a decree that all people fear and tremble before this marvelous God who Daniel worshipped and served. Daniel, having earned respect, continued to enjoy success during his days of living among people who did not know God (Daniel 6:1-28).

Another thing that helped Daniel survive in a non-Christian culture were friends who believed in the same God (Daniel 2:17-18). It is wise to make sure we do what we can to have close believers in our lives who serve as a source of strength, encouragement, and help (Proverbs 27:17). Jesus, too, had a group to whom he looked to be with in difficult times and with whom he shared his intimate concerns (Mark 14:32-34; John 15:12-17). Responsible Christian living and strength for survival is greatly enhanced when we connect with a loving-one-another fellowship of believers. To be part of Christ's body, called the church, is a safe place to be because Jesus said he was building his church and not even the gates of Hades could overpower it (Matthew 16:18). According to God's promises, Christ's church (as well as believing Israel) will one day triumph over the evils that have tried to destroy them. Such is our sustaining hope in troublesome times.

CHOOSING TO SUFFER WITH GOD'S PEOPLE

Should persecution deter me from choosing to follow Jesus? Moses grew up in an Egyptian pharaoh's household that was unfavorable toward God and his people (Exodus 2:1-15). The scriptures say Moses refused to be part of the lifestyle of that culture, and even though he might suffer persecution, "he chose rather to endure ill-treatment with the people of God than to enjoy the passing pleasures of sin, considering the reproach of Christ greater riches than the treasures of Egypt; for he was looking to the reward" (Hebrews 11:24-26). Rather than enjoying and joining the ways of an ungodly world, a firm choice he made when living in an ungodly society was to join with the people of God, facing the cost of possible suffering, knowing the hope that God has something better planned for his people. Moses thought about God and what God offered, and he developed an attitude toward suffering. He determined that *God's riches and rewards are greater than the world's riches and rewards.*

If we would follow Jesus into his persecutions (Mark 10:28-30), an essential place to start would be to check our *attitude toward suffering.* Attitude is our mental or emotional position or stand toward any person, place, thing, or event. Attitudes determine motivation, choices, and the direction our life will take. Attitudes can be positive or negative and will determine whether we will make good progress in our lives or come to ruin.

What attitudes do you see in the persons portrayed in this chapter? For example, the attitude of the woman who was going to die in a famine (*I am OK with dying*), or Joseph's attitude toward the bad things that happened to him (*I will wait upon God, be patient, and make the best of my circumstances*), or the attitude of Moses as mentioned above. What attitude do you have toward taking a stand for God even if it means suffering? Such attitudes (good or bad) might include any of the following:

- "Following Christ is important, and I want to learn and prepare for what may come."

- "I'll deal with it when I need to; meanwhile, it's business as usual for me."

- "It scares me to think about it, so I don't."

- "I could never have faith that is strong enough."

- "I am not willing to suffer for my faith."

- "I could never show God's love for my persecutors."

- "Even if persecuted, I am going to give what it takes to love and meets others' needs."

- "My faith in God's wisdom, that he knows what he is doing, will keep me afloat in any situation."

- "God can bring good out of bad situations."

- "Christ in the center of my life will be my stability in the midst of chaos and confusion."

Right attitudes motivate my direction and must come first if the foes of my life are to be defeated. What is your attitude toward suffering? What is mine? Do I need to make an adjustment in my attitude? How can my attitude be changed?

Along with checking our attitudes about following Jesus into his sufferings, it is good to consider what *deeds or actions we can practice* that will demonstrate Christian faith, hope, and love. For example, in this chapter we have seen the practices of Daniel (*I will wisely influence people, even those who want me to join them in doing something God does not want me to do*), or Ebed-melech (*I see something I will do to help a person in need*). When it comes to being an effective witness for God in any culture, we can decide to appropriately serve those whom

God places in our lives and to work hard to help them achieve their goals (if their goals are not evil). In countries where Christians are suffering painful social rejections and sometimes physical hostility, they have learned that loving the neighboring people around them, and even their enemies, is causing many to see what the love of Jesus is like, and many are turning to Christ for his kind of life—a life they are not seeing or experiencing from their own religions or cultures.

Naturally we must consider how we are being received. By sensing an open or closed heart toward us, we can determine how best to proceed. Some persons may be favorable toward us, and we may lead them to Jesus by loving and serving and being a blessing to them. But not everyone will be favorable toward us, and we may have to suffer their evils. In such cases we must learn to overcome our fears of what mankind can do to us. To give us courage in the presence of fear, we will need the kind of hope we receive from God's Word. When people around us witness our hope and see how powerful it is to give us peace in the midst of suffering, it increases their desire for the Christian way of life.

Finally, *in what areas does God want to grow me* so I can be his good news in a bad news world? Am I earnestly praying for God to help me to be who I need to be and to do those things that will bring the hope of life to others and glory to God? One of the key actions we can practice to enable us to grow in love and hope is to receive needed strength, encouragement, support, and prayer by being in close fellowship with our brothers and sisters in Christ. I have discovered that if I want to grow in a certain area of my Christian life, my best success comes when I team up with one or more persons who want the same in their lives (Proverbs 27:17). For example, I wanted to grow in my ability to talk to others about spiritual things so I could be more than just an example, although I know being an example is often the best way to communicate my faith. A good friend wanted to learn to do the same, so for a year we met each week to discuss ways to do it. We would pray, encourage each other to talk to someone during the week, and share what happened when we met the next week. It was amazing how many opportunities God gave us to talk about spiritual things with people we came in contact with. It did not happen every week, but it happened much more than if we were trying to do it by ourselves (Ecclesiastes 4:9-10). It was always on our minds to be praying and looking for opportunities. When we can be with other believers and help each other grow in love and prepare for suffering by talking about what it means to have hope, we have a powerful resource for overcoming our troublesome times (Hebrews 10:23-25). In the next chapter we consider what kind of life God calls us to live if we are to be his good news and bearers of hope.

CHAPTER 5

FIVE WAYS TO LIVE AS HOPE-FILLED CHRISTIANS IN A NON-CHRISTIAN CULTURE

Paul, a man appointed by God to be an ambassador for the Savior of the world, wrote two letters to a church in Thessalonica, an ancient port city in northern Greece. During Paul's short visit to their city, a church was born, but it was left to survive in an environment of threatening opposition and persecution (1 Thessalonians 1:6; 2:2, 14-16; 2 Thessalonians 1:4-5). It all began in a Jewish synagogue when Paul pointed out from the Old Testament scriptures that their promised Messiah had to suffer, die, and be bodily raised from the dead, thus giving all mankind an opportunity not to die but to enter God's kingdom. Paul proclaimed Jesus as that Messiah. Some were persuaded and believed, but others formed a mob and set the city in an uproar. They dragged one of the believers from his home, rounded up a few others, and brought them before the city officials. They stirred up the crowd by accusing them of being troublemakers who proclaimed allegiance to another king and who opposed the laws of the emperor. Concerned for Paul's safety, the believers urged him to get out of the city, but he had to wait until dark (Acts 17:1-10). These Thessalonian letters were written to instruct, strengthen, and encourage the new believers to remain faithful as they continued to suffer persecution from their fellow countrymen (1 Thessalonians 3:2-4).

One night, I decided to read these two letters to discover what Paul had to say about how to live in a society opposed to hearing God's Word (actually, we are to live in these ways as best we can all the time). I listed at least thirty-eight ways Paul taught them to live in the midst of their non-accepting society, and after mulling over the list, I combined those items into five positive instructions prescribing how to be God's light in a world of darkness (Ephesians 5:8). The five instructions are these: (1) take care of your soul, (2) love all people, (3) stand firm in the faith, (4) live holy lives, and (5) hope in Christ. These are God's instructions for living the Christian life in a community prone to look upon Christianity with disfavor. God wants us to grow in our works of faith, labors of love, and steadfastness of hope (1 Thessalonians 1:3).

Here then are five ways to live our lives in a society that does not know our God. This would make a good group Bible study for discussing what this lifestyle means for you.

TAKE CARE OF YOUR SOUL

God is the ultimate caretaker of our soul, for he created us and wants us to be good bearers of his image (Romans 8:29). But we must cooperate with him in this. To take care of our soul involves taking inventory of where our life stands with God. For example, *Is my thinking in line with God's thinking? Is my lifestyle honoring to him?* God has a very good reason for us to be taking care of our souls. There is a saying that if you don't take care of yourself, you are no good for anyone else. God would have us care not just about self but also about others (Matthew 22:37-39; Philippians 2:4). If you care about being there for people you love and for neighbors and friends and strangers who need help, you can better offer them what they need (physically, mentally, socially, spiritually) if you take care of yourself along the way.

What does caring for our soul involve? The Greek word in the New Testament translated as "soul" is the word *psuche*, from which we get our word *psychology*, a branch of science dealing with the mind and its influence on our behaviors. This inner part of our being includes emotions such as love, anger, hatred, guilt, anxiety, worry, peace, joy, desire, and so forth. The inner life also includes intellect, which involves thinking, planning, and deciding, which then involves the will to act, which then determines our outward behaviors. When we examine our thoughts, are we taken up with mostly negative or positive thoughts, good or bad thoughts, right or wrong thoughts, angry thoughts, worrisome thoughts, happy thoughts, or God's thoughts? (Philippians 4:8).

The word *soul* not only refers to our inner life of emotions, thinking, and will but is sometimes used to refer to the whole person: body, soul, and spirit. It's important to consider the direction our whole life is going because we have children, a spouse, extended family, friends, neighbors, jobs, a social life, a church, God's work, health, money, and household tasks to maintain. Life has many responsibilities, and we must learn to balance them so the needs of each one are being adequately tended to. We take inventory of our inner life so as to keep our whole life on track. This includes knowing our purpose, mission, aim, or goal as followers of Jesus. Where is he leading us?

Certainly figuring out and becoming the people God has designed us to be is part of soul care. The inner workings of the human being can be a mystery difficult to understand. Self-examination is something the Bible encourages as a way to help us understand who we are (Genesis 4:6-7; Psalm 139:23-24; Lamentations 3:40; Acts 24:16; 1 John 1:9). But to avoid getting lost in introspection, we rely on outside sources. We rely on God's Holy Spirit to provide insights through his Word (Psalm 119:99, 105, 130), and we listen to other people, seeking to discern the truth of what they say. We do not necessarily have to agree with what people say, but the rebukes, reproofs, or words of those who know us best should be respected and considered if needed change is to take place (Proverbs 23:22-23; 27:5-6; Romans 15:14).

I read the words of one family counselor who pointed out that he would counsel a lot fewer marriage problems if each partner would listen to their spouse's well-meaning criticisms. As Christians, we take care of our soul when we desire and seek true insights into ourselves, good and evil, and learn to rely on God to help us change (Psalm 51:10; Proverbs 3:5-6). Soul care is learning from God who we are and then seeking to live accordingly.

Paul had a fear that these new believers would fail to remain true to God when suffering under the afflictions of their persecutors (1 Thessalonians 3:4-5). Our soul is in danger of taking a wrong turn when experiencing the temptations, evils, hardships, and sufferings of this world (Mark 4:16-17). In troublesome times, the very core of our being can be shaken with doubts, fears, and anxieties. Confused about what to believe or do, we are easily tempted to listen and give in to our emotions and other voices telling us to do or believe the wrong things.

One of the ways Paul shows his personal concern for the inner and whole life of the believers (1 Thessalonians 2:8) is by telling them of his prayers for them. Because they are suffering afflictions due to persecution, Paul prays that God will *comfort* them and *strengthen their hearts* and that they will *realize the hope* they have been given from God (2 Thessalonians 2:16-17). Paul also recognizes their God-given *desire for goodness* and prays that these desires can be fulfilled for the glory of God (2 Thessalonians 1:11-12). These are soul care issues, and Paul lets them know that to possess things like comfort, strength of heart, realization of hope, and the goodness needed for works of faith, one must grow the inner life by seeking God and his resources. To omit the Spirit's power and wise counsel can be very costly (Proverbs 1:29-33).

What is it that Paul says will enable the new believers' lives to grow and be strong in the face of their sufferings? He would say we must rely on God by believing and practicing the truths he tells us. His Spirit-inspired letters aim at some of those truths. For example, they were reminded of the truth that they have been chosen and loved by God (1 Thessalonians 1:4; 2 Thessalonians 2:13). When internalized, the truth of God's love and acceptance brings healing and strength to the troubled soul. Being loved means God cares about us and will keep us safe from evils that seek to destroy us (Psalm 16:8-9; 40:1-17; 2

Thessalonians 3:3). Even in death we are safe, for nothing can separate us from God's love (1 Thessalonians 5:9-10). Through these truths, by God's grace, we can receive comfort, hope, and strength, enabling us to endure hardships and faithfully continue to live out our daily callings to engage in God's good works (2 Thessalonians 2:16-17).[10] Paul reminds us that we take care of our soul when we continue in prayerfulness about everything, asking and trusting God for his grace to help us (1 Thessalonians 5:17). We also take care of our soul when we allow God to work his will in us, choosing to hold fast to that which is good and to abstain from every form of evil (1 Thessalonians 5:19-22). These and other statements in Paul's letters give us ways to take care of our soul.

I was at a park one day, and I noticed an elderly woman sitting alone on a park bench, so I walked over and sat down. We conversed for a bit, and then, evidently sensing that I was a safe person to talk to, she began to share parts of her life story. She told me of horrendous abuses as a child, followed by many bitter and heartbreaking events throughout her adult life. She was now suffering very severe health problems and many broken relationships—most of them, she admitted, were the result of her own bad choices. Not knowing I was a person of faith, she began sharing how she met God and how the Bible is now a most valuable possession in her life. She said that whenever she is having a problem mentally, emotionally, or physically, she reads her Bible and has found it to be life-giving. She shared how the words of God speak to her and help her. Whether she needs comfort, peace of mind, encouragement, or guidance, the Bible calms her and gives her just what she needs at the time. Hearing her story, I felt warmed and encouraged in my faith. In this woman's life, God was fulfilling his Word to redeem, free, comfort, and bring gladness to the brokenhearted and to those who mourn (Isaiah 61:1-3). Her story is a good illustration of 1 Thessalonians 2:13, which says, "You received the word of God which performs its work in you who believe."

---

10. Bruce Wilkinson, with David Kopp, *You Were Born for This* (Colorado Springs, CO: Multnomah Books, 2009). This is an amazing book showing how we as believers can step out in faith each day and see God's miracles in people whose lives we touch by meeting their needs.

This woman's relationship with God and to God's Word is not unique. God's Book of history, poetry, letters, teachings, and promises is very instrumental in the care of our soul. Sincere believers rely on God and his Word to receive ongoing care (Psalm 119:49-50; 1 Peter 2:2). I was recently reminded of a statement someone made: "The Bible is the only book whose author is always present when it is read." As we read the Bible and reflect carefully on the personal qualities of God and on what he does for us, our confidence in him grows to an unshakable trust in him, no matter what (Psalm 73:21-28). This knowledge and reliance on God allows us to receive his gracious love, peace, and steadfastness in the midst of turmoil, enabling us to rejoice always and to be thankful in everything (1 Thessalonians 5:16, 18; 2 Thessalonians 3:5, 16, 18). We take care of our soul when we are into God's Word, believing and practicing what he says (1 Thessalonians 2:13).

Notice that Paul encourages the believers to read his letters to each other (1 Thessalonians 5:27; Colossians 4:16). For my own life (and I know many Christians feel the same way), I find it absolutely essential to go to God's Word every day and especially in times when I feel weak or confused and in need of strength, peace, and guidance. It's easy to lose our way amidst the pressures and demands of daily life. I like to tell busy people that even if you read a verse or two a day and think about it, you will gain and benefit.

What did we just discover from these letters about ways to take care of our soul? Perhaps it would solidify some things in our minds if we went back, underlined, and thought about how we are practicing them.

LOVE ALL PEOPLE

Paul instructs the Thessalonian believers to abound in love for one another and for all people (1 Thessalonians 3:12). Loving all people, even our enemies, is what Jesus wants us to do, for as Jesus reminds us, God is good to all, both the evil and the good. One way we love and practice good to those who persecute us is to pray for them (Matthew 5:43-48). Pray that God will reach and change them with his kindness and that he will help you to know how to be part of what he wants to do in their lives.

I admire my wife. People are drawn to her because she listens and cares. She shows God's kindness to all kinds of people by writing them encouraging notes or noticing good and positive things they do and telling them she appreciates that. She also is constantly meeting needs she has picked up on through observations or conversations with people—for example, the time she gave a homeless person gloves for the cold weather. Loving your fellow believers is also huge, for loving one another as God loves is what distinguishes us as followers of Jesus (John 13:35). When people notice love, they may wish for and begin to seek that kind of relationship for themselves.

But what does love mean? Unfortunately, in the American culture, many have come to believe love is a sentimental feeling that caters to the desires of others by giving them what they want and by accepting their lifestyles and actions without qualification or judgment. One command in the Bible believed by many non-Christians, and one they are quick to remind Christians about, is "Do not judge" (Matthew 7:1). It is easy for all of us to be confused about the Bible's teachings on judgment and thus fail to distinguish between being judgmental and making sound judgments. Our society makes lots and lots of laws about everything: warning labels on cigarette packages, speed limits on highways, legal marriages, murder, robbery, health care, minimum wages, minority rights, and on and on. Whether or not we all agree with the laws, what this tells us is that people share a common belief in the existence of right and wrong. Law courts daily make judgments about whether or not someone has broken a law. This does not mean the judges are being judgmental. Being judgmental as we commonly use the term has the connotation of putting people down by unfairly or undeservedly condemning and not accepting them. We can easily base our treatment of them on our likes or dislikes instead of on knowing enough about them to make accurate judgments. Naturally, we may have an intuition about some people, but depending on the situation, it may be best to keep our intuition to ourselves and use it as a caution until we get to know them better.

The point of this brief digression about love and judgment is that we can easily misunderstand the love of God and what it means to love others as God loves them. Judgment is very much a part of

God's love. D. A. Carson, in his book *The Difficult Doctrine of the Love of God*, has gleaned from scripture at least five aspects or ways the Bible speaks of God's love and how we distort the love of God because we do not know God as he has revealed himself.[11] Jesus, our supreme example of God's love, makes a judgment when he tells others the truth about themselves (for example Matthew 21:23-46; John 8:39-47). He was not being judgmental in doing so. In fact, another statement of his is, "Do not judge according to appearance, but judge with righteous judgment" (John 7:24). I am not suggesting it is OK to be making judgments about everyone, especially those outside the faith. We often do not know enough or are not kind enough to do it properly and rightly, but the Bible does give permission, particularly to believers in the faith, to judge one another (1 Corinthians 5:9-13; 6:1-3).

It goes without saying that we believers are to love others and to excel still more, increasing and abounding in love for one another and for all people (1 Thessalonians 3:12; 4:9-10). Oops, maybe it does need saying, because judging by the way we Christians in churches often treat each other and outsiders, it is apparent love is a very difficult character quality to consistently practice. It may help us do better if we consider the importance of loving one another. With the daily problems we all face and especially in a contrary society, it is important to build up and strengthen one another so we can persevere through tough times.

Paul's letters tell us what it means to love one another. Love is doing what is good for others, and he describes what is good in the following ways:

- "Encourage one another and build up one another" (1 Thessalonians 5:11).

- "Appreciate those who labor among you, live in peace with one another, admonish the unruly, encourage the fainthearted, help the weak, be patient with everyone, and do not repay another with evil for evil, but always seek after that which is good for one another and for all people" (1 Thessalonians 5:12-15).

---

11. D. A. Carson, *The Difficult Doctrine of the Love of God* (Wheaton, Illinois: Crossway, 2000).

- Admonish anyone who is not following the instructions of God's Word: "Do not regard him as an enemy, but admonish him as a brother" (2 Thessalonians 3:14-15).

- "Do not grow weary in doing good" (2 Thessalonians 3:13).

First Corinthians 13:3-7 further defines love, especially in the context of using our God-given gifts to meet one another's needs. Loving in these ways takes conscious effort and is not something we can do on our own. That is why Paul prays, "May the Lord cause you to love" (1 Thessalonians 3:12), and, "May the Lord direct your hearts into the love of God (2 Thessalonians 3:5). We've already made the point about taking care of our souls. A great way to take care of our souls is to recognize our need for love and to pray often for God to help us love as he loves: with wisdom, grace, and truth.

STAND FIRM IN THE FAITH

Paul says in 1 Thessalonians 3:8, "Stand firm in the Lord." In the midst of distress and affliction, a firm faith will stand out and strengthen onlookers (1 Thessalonians 3:7-8). The Bible's comment that we walk by faith and not by sight (2 Corinthians 5:7) is necessary when life becomes dark. Sometimes during a storm, the electric power in our house is cut off. Darkness needs to be overcome, and a flashlight or candlelight becomes handy. The light enables me to see and keeps me from taking missteps and falling. So it is with faith in our lives. In a world of ungodliness and empty hopes, one's faith stands out as a light in a dark place.

The church people Paul is writing to are to be commended for the stand they are taking for God in the midst of an anti-God community. Those outside their faith notice that they have turned from their idols and their former way of life to serve a living and true God (1 Thessalonians 1:9). They see these people attending gatherings with other Christians instead of their previous routine of worshiping in the pagan temples. They see these believers loving one another in ways that were not true in their former relationships. They see these believers sacrificially practicing good deeds to those outside the faith, whether to former friends, or acquaintances, or even to strangers, and it becomes clear that these believers love others. Their unwavering faith and commitment toward God has been noticed by people far and wide (1 Thessalonians 1:8-9).

People could see a difference in their lives. They lived a different lifestyle from the world and could tell others what made the difference. They not only lived differently, but they endured their trials with the hope of eternal life in Christ. They had accepted their sufferings as part of what it meant to follow Jesus, and they did this with the joy of the Holy Spirit (1 Thessalonians 1:6). Standing firm in the faith meant for them that it would be foolish to give up their faith and fall back to their old ways of living (Romans 6:21-22).

We stand firm in the faith when we are confident of our salvation (1 Thessalonians 1:5; 5:8-10). During a conversation, a person who did not know I was a Christian said to me, "Christians *think* they are saved and going to heaven." I responded from my own position as a Christian by saying, "No, they don't *think* so, they know so." He repeated that they *think* so, and I countered that they *know* so. He finally conceded, "Ok, this is something believers know to be true" (1 John 5:13).

Knowing something without doubt enables one to stand firm in the face of opposition. "Stand firm and hold to the traditions you were taught," Paul told them (2 Thessalonians 2:15). Those traditions consisted of the words of truth passed down to them by those who witnessed the death, burial, and resurrection of Christ Jesus. They were convinced the message Paul brought to them was the truth because the gospel came to them—not in eyewitnessed word only, but in the power of the Holy Spirit who drew them to God, came to live in them, and changed them (John 1:12-13; 3:3-8; Acts 2:38-39; 1 Peter 1:22-23). These believers had become part of a worldwide group that had been prophesied, unknowingly, by an enemy of Jesus, who said "that Jesus was going to die . . . in order that He might also gather together into one the children of God who are scattered abroad" (John 11:51-52).

That prophecy came true as Jesus' death has resulted in people from all over the world becoming children of God (1 John 3:1-2; Revelation 5:9). The gospel, the message of the story of Jesus, was true. It was not the word of men but was the word of God because it did a marvelous work in their lives (1 Thessalonians 1:5; 2:13).

One of the works that accepting the truth of the gospel did in these Thessalonian believers was to enable them to stand firm in the face of sufferings at the hands of their countrymen (1 Thessalonians 2:14). Nothing could convince them that another way of life was better, for whether they lived or died, they knew they would live together with Jesus (1 Thessalonians 5:10).

Paul had to leave these new Christians when he fled the city. As mentioned above, he prayed earnestly for them because he feared they would give up their faith under persecution. But when he found out that they were persevering and their faith was growing stronger, their firm stand in the faith caused Paul's heart to rejoice and praise God's faithfulness (1 Thessalonians 3:1-9).

When our fellow brothers and sisters in the faith see that we stand firm through our difficult or life-threatening trials, they are encouraged and strengthened to do the same. This is not to say we don't have our weak moments, but when people see us work through them and become stronger, it shows the soundness of our faith. We can honestly let them know our weak feelings, but we can assure them that greater is he who is in us than he who is in the world (1 John 4:4). In times of affliction at the hands of others, we pray for God's protection, and we trust that his protection surrounds us— whether it be in the form of helping us escape our persecutors or giving us courage, peace, and joy in the midst of it (Acts 7:54-60; 2 Thessalonians 3:3, 5; Revelation 3:8-12). Paul prayed for these believers that Jesus would be glorified in them (2 Thessalonians 1:11-12), and it was answered as these believers honored the name of Jesus by how they believed and lived (2 Thessalonians 1:3-5).

LIVE HOLY LIVES

God has declared us holy through faith in his forgiveness, which was made possible by the sacrifice of Jesus on the cross. But until we possess our future righteous bodies, imperfections still inhabit our earthly ones. When Paul says to these Thessalonians to be holy, he therefore means for them to cleanse themselves from the defilements of flesh and spirit (2 Corinthians 7:1). Defilement means we become dirty or unclean in God's sight by thoughts or actions that fall short of the perfect, evil-free nature of God. Jesus taught about defilement when he said what comes out of the heart of a person is what defiles the person. Then he mentioned a list of thoughts and actions that define defilement (Mark 7:14-23).

There are two ways to be holy before God. The first way is to be forgiven. We have believed, have been baptized, and have become one with Christ Jesus, whose death on the cross cleanses us from all sin. We are clean when forgiven through our faith in the gospel promises. Thereafter, when we commit any sins, we remain clean by confessing our wrongs and believing God's forgiveness (1 John 1:5-10; 2:1-2).[12]

The second way to be holy before God is to practice right living. Paul expresses what it means to be holy with the words, "to walk and please God" (1 Thessalonians 4:1). He writes, "God has not called us for the purpose of impurity, but in sanctification" (1 Thessalonians 4:3). *Sanctification* is a big word, and it comes from the same word as *holy*. It means that God has called us to be set apart for his purposes. In the context here, the will and purpose of God for Christians is to abstain from sexual impurity. To reject living a holy life is to reject God, who gives his Holy Spirit to us (1 Thessalonians 4:8). Regarding our sexuality, we know that God has created us as sexual beings, and used properly, sexual activity is a good and wonderful gift from God. But using our sexuality in the wrong ways is not fitting behavior to a holy God. We need to have self-control, which is a fruit of God's Spirit, and not give way to lustful passions like the people who do not know God (Romans 13:14; Galatians 5:16, 22-23). Purity of life was important for these Thessalonian believers, for they lived in a culture, just as we do today, where sexual impurity was rampant. It was another way of showing the difference between a follower of Jesus and people of the world.

Another area in living a holy life is in your day-to-day work. Earlier in this book we noticed the admirable work habits of Joseph and Daniel and how the honorable way they worked led to God giving them favor in the eyes of their bosses. Here,

---

12. Much more needs to be understood about sin in the believer's life than I have presented here. I refer you to the Apostle Paul's teaching in Romans 5–8. I cover the subject more fully in a previous book, *Out of Darkness into the Light*, chapter 16: "How Christians need to think about sin in their lives," pages 164–174.

Paul admonishes the Christians to be responsible and work, for many were not working and were getting into trouble with their idle time (1 Thessalonians 4:11-12; 2 Thessalonians 3:7-12). They were depending on others to support them instead of pulling their weight in society. Being idle and bothering people by interfering in their business was neither holy nor the loving way to behave toward family or others in the community.

In the context of these verses, some have said that those who were not working may have been thinking, *Why work if Jesus is coming back soon?* Many of us have heard the saying that "we can be so heavenly-minded we are no earthly good." That applies here. The truth is, if we are heavenly-minded, we should be *more* earthly good, for the present earthly realm is where Jesus sends us to represent him. The believers were to work to earn their living and not be a burden on others.

To summarize God's will for holy living, the Bible is specific in telling us of our need to be purifying ourselves so we can be holy as God is holy (Leviticus 11:44-45; James 4:8; 1 Peter 1:15-16; 2 Peter 3:10-14; 1 John 3:3). Being pure begins with a new God-given heart and dedicating our lives to God's will.

HOPE IN CHRIST

Paul's Thessalonian letters have a lot to say about what the world is coming to, including Jesus' return to earth. These believers looked forward to Jesus coming because it meant at least the following four things: (1) being rescued from God's wrath on the Day of Judgment; (2) the resurrection of their bodies; (3) being with Jesus and other believers in the kingdom of God; and (4) relief from unjust persecutions and sufferings (1 Thessalonians 1:10, 4:13-17; 2 Thessalonians 1:6-8; Revelation 6:9-11). They are guaranteed this fourfold hope because God is faithful, and he will bring it to pass, for God has chosen them "for salvation through sanctification by the Spirit, and faith in the truth" (1 Thessalonians 5:24; 2 Thessalonians 2:13).

These words of hope may not seem to be very meaningful to you, but if your troublesome times are defined by persecution, as it was for these Thessalonians and for many in our world today, then they are words that give the suffering soul needed comfort and help to persevere. It was during the harsh days of war when the extreme persecution of Jews and others, including some Christians who stood against this evil, was taking place that C. S. Lewis reminded God's people of the importance of focusing on their hope. He wrote, "Hope means that a continual looking forward to the eternal world is not (as some modern people think) a form of escapism or wishful thinking, but one of the things a Christian is meant to do." He says we have not been trained to focus on heaven because "our whole education tends to fix our minds on this world." He says, "I must keep alive in myself the desire for my true country . . . I must make it the main object of life to press on to that other country and to help others to do the same." Why? He answers, "If you read history you will find that the Christians who did the most for the present world were just those who thought most of the next."[13] With these thoughts, the Bible agrees (Philippians 3:7-14; Colossians 3:2; Hebrews 11:8-10, 13-16).

MOTIVATION FOR PRACTICING THESE FIVE ADMONITIONS

The maturing Thessalonian Christians were naturally living out these admonitions as their new way of life because Christ's Spirit was in them. I realize there are some who feel greatly burdened by the thought of *having* to practice all these commands and teachings of God. Some become atheists to get out from under the weight of having to live as God wants. They feel free when they can eliminate the guilt placed on them by failing to live up to God's standards. Even some Christians feel living the Christian life is a duty, and they get tired of trying to live up to its commands or rules. Understandably, with that viewpoint, Christianity would be impossible to enjoy. That would be equivalent to living under Old Testament Law—which often leads to legalism, fear of judgment, and faking one's faith so as to appear good. But that is not how life in Christ is lived.

---

13. C. S. Lewis, *Mere Christianity* (New York: Macmillan Publishing Co., 1943, 1945, 1952), 118-120.

Having received a changed heart with God's Spirit put within me, I live in the grace of God, and I feel constantly affirmed by God, even in my failures to measure up. Rather than feeling burdened by God's design for right living, I feel I *want* to live by his prescribed ways because of his love for me and my love for him. I want to grow to become the best person I can be, and I believe God is the person who best defines what that means. I am not overwhelmed by these five ways to live my life for they are a natural part of how my heart is now programed to live. Plus, I do not have to put myself down for failing to mature as fast as I would like. Knowing his forgiveness, I accept myself with my imperfections because he accepts me. I do not live under any guilt because all of that has been removed at the cross of Christ. I humbly confess any wrongs, receive forgiveness, and move forward. God is patient and gentle with me, though persistent in his reminders that I need to keep maturing by working on certain areas of my life. Intentionally worked out in my life, with the much-needed help of fellow believers, the five above-mentioned ways to live will please and honor God, will help me survive in a Godless culture until he comes, will give meaning and purpose to my life, and will allow God to bring others into his kingdom through my faithfulness to his cause (Matthew 11:28-30; Philippians 2:12-13; 1:6).

CHAPTER 6

WHAT CAN WE EXPECT IN THE NEXT LIFE?

I am sitting outside, admiring my surroundings, and I begin thinking about leaving this earth. The thought of it creates a deep-felt sadness and emptiness in me, for I love the beauty of God's creation: the trees and rustling of leaves, the songs of birds, the rolling, plant-covered landscapes, the fascinating ways of animals, the sunrises, the sunsets, and the cloud formations, the wonder of the stars, the vivid colors of delicately formed flowers, gentle rains, flowing rivers, cascading creeks, and sky-mirroring lakes. I feel quieted and renewed by the still hush of woods and forests, the rare absolute silence when alone on the prairies, and the refreshing feel of wind blowing across my face. It is awe-inspiring to see majestic mountains, whether clothed in brilliant sunlight or in the gray shadows of foggy mists. I even love the startling thunder-clapping storms that remind me of God's unmatchable power. All of this has been a part of my earth-bound experience. I have become attached; I don't want to leave it.

Then I think that I should not hate to leave; I should not hold on to these things of nature because they are not the most important things in life (1 John 2:15-17). I am not down-playing the fact that above all I desire to be with God and my beloved Jesus and with loved ones, but why shouldn't I feel this way about leaving the earth I live in? After all, God made me to be a part of nature, created from the *stuff* of the ground (Genesis 2:7). I know that God has a better place for us, but in my limited vision, I can't imagine anything better than a planet like this, designed and given by God to sustain life, full of breathtaking beauty and interesting diversity, offering much to discover and marvel at and use and enjoy. Earth is the home God made for us.

Then, as I read the Bible, rather than grieving the loss of my life on earth, I become confident that I will gain much more. It seems apparent that the Bible gives us an unfailing hope that invisible immaterial—*soul stuff*—and visible material—*physical stuff*—which are bound together in this life, will remain bound together in the world to come. In fact, they will have similarities to our present world, minus the defects of evil and corruption. My spirit of loss and sadness becomes excited and joyful when I contemplate the hope that our bodies will be resurrected from the dead and we will dwell on a new earth that has similarities to our present experiences. Explore with me some of the things the Bible says we can expect in the coming ages of the world: a new body, righteousness, life on a new earth, fulfilling work, and our blessed hope.

THE RESURRECTED BODY

Does the Bible say the human body in the next life will be a combination of what I call "soul stuff" and "physical stuff"? An unexpected event happened in history. The Gospels record things about the resurrected body of Jesus. After Jesus was crucified, dead, and buried, his tomb was found empty, and he appeared in bodily form to his followers (Luke 24:1-12, 36-43). I know many would say, at least before quantum discoveries, that *scientifically speaking*, this cannot happen, but science does not control what can or cannot happen in history. History has its own methods of evidential proof. The eyewitnessed resurrected body of Jesus (1 Corinthians 15:3-8) convinces us that after death, a physical body can live again—that *soul stuff* and *physical stuff* can be reunited (John 11:25-26). True, the resurrected body of Jesus was different than his earthly body, yet in some aspects it was the same. It was different in that it could mysteriously appear and disappear, pass through walls or closed doors (Luke 24:30-31; John 20:26),[14] and no longer die (Romans 6:9). But even though Jesus' resurrected body is different, and even though he may not have been readily recognizable, his body *was* capable of being recognized by those who saw him (Luke 24:13-31; John 21:12). His body could be visibly present and touchable, could eat, and had flesh and bones as we all have (Luke 24:39, 41-43). In some way, *soul stuff* and *physical stuff* remained connected. As believers, we have the certain hope that when he appears again, our bodies will be resurrected and become like his glorious body (1 Corinthians 6:14; 1 Thessalonians 4:13-18; Philippians 3:20-21). God meant for the whole man—body, soul, spirit—to be preserved forever (1 Thessalonians 5:23).

The nature of the resurrected body is further described in 1 Corinthians 15. Again, it is pointed out that we will be raised bodily just as Christ Jesus was raised bodily. Jesus is the first fruit (the beginning of a new kind of humanity), showing what our human body will be like when we are raised from the dead (1 Corinthians 15:16-23). Our new body will no longer perish, no longer be dishonorable, and no longer be weak; rather, it will be imperishable and of honorable character and will possess a new power to live a righteous life (1 Corinthians 15:42-43). Then comes an intriguing concept: it is no longer a *natural* body but a *spiritual* body (1 Corinthians 15:44). The term *spiritual body* does not mean a ghost-like spirit without any physical stuff involved. No! A spiritual body means that it is a body that is no longer corrupted by evil but designed to live free of sin and death in the coming new world. It is a body possessing the moral qualities of spiritual life found in God's kingdom.

Already, due to a spiritual birth motivating us to practice Jesus' teachings in our present earthly life (John 3:5-6), we are being transformed from one degree of glory to another (2 Corinthians 3:18). The likeness of Christ is being formed in us (Romans 8:29; Galatians 4:19; 1 John 3:2-3), and a new body, fit to live as God intends, is forthcoming.

---

14. Jesus said his realm was not of this world (John 18:36). Things reported about him, like appearing and disappearing, passing through solid walls, and going instantly from one place to another (John 6:21) are visible signs that he truly was from another dimension. If you are familiar with the issues scientists wrestle with in their study of quantum physics, you will realize that discoveries and repeated experiments in quantum physics make these reports about Jesus very believable.

It is called a spiritual body because it is ever under the guidance and influence of the Spirit of God. A spiritual body is one like Jesus has—one that will never die, able to live a perfect godly life, and yet still can be connected with *physical stuff*. I know that some have questioned a physical body in heaven based on 1 Corinthians 15:50. It says, "flesh and blood cannot inherit the kingdom of God." This phrase taken in its present context does refer to our earthly bodies, but they are bodies controlled by a fleshly sinful nature, which in that condition do not understand the things of God and fight against God's spiritual nature (1 Corinthians 2:14; Galatians 5:16-26). Such a nature is not fit for life in God's kingdom, where there is no sin (1 Corinthians 15:17). Instead of earthly bodies controlled by our sinful nature, we need heavenly bodies controlled by our spiritual nature. Thus the body is described in 1 Corinthians 15 as a spiritual body, one possessing a spiritual nature, one that cannot sin.

Some groups, like Gnostics, believe that material stuff is evil and that nothing physical can exist in our life after death; therefore, we will live in another world as pure spirits. But the material body is not evil unless evil has infiltrated and corrupted it. God created matter as good, and he will one day set his material creation free from its corruption (Romans 8:19-21). To say that flesh and blood cannot inherit the kingdom of God is true because our present body is sinful, perishable, and dishonorable, and in that condition, cannot go to heaven. But the heavenly body is raised as an imperishable and honorable body, no longer controlled by a sinful nature, but possessing the life of the Spirit of God (Romans 6:4-6; 8:5-11).

In summary, what can we expect in the next life regarding our human body? The Bible promises a continuation of our physical bodies, and although they are different from our present bodies, they maintain similarity to the ones we have in our present world. Undoubtedly, like Jesus' body, our bodies will be able to perform things in the next world not normally done in this world. It will be a different world after all, but Christians have the hope of a redeemed, newly perfected, and eternally existing body like Christ's (Romans 8:23-25; 1 Corinthians 6:14; Philippians 3:20-21), with our personal identity still preserved, recognized, and able to communicate with a personal God and with each other.

THE HOPE OF RIGHTEOUSNESS

The Bible tells us we have the hope of righteousness (Galatians 5:5). By our faith in Christ and God's promises, we can know God has declared us *not guilty*, free from the condemnation of laws we could not keep, and free from a bothersome conscience (Romans 8:1; Hebrews 10:22). We are forgiven and accepted in God's sight. He has *pronounced* us righteous (Romans 4). And when we enter the next age, we *will be* righteous (free from sin) and live in a righteous world. Psalm 125:3 tells us that "the scepter of wickedness shall not rest upon the land of the righteous, so that the righteous will not put forth their hands to do wrong." Can you imagine what it will be like to no longer struggle against evil thoughts, hatred for people, or fear of being abused or robbed or physically harmed? Can you imagine what it will be like to no longer be overcome by temptations causing us to fall again into life-destroying habits? No longer having to beat yourself up for hurting people you love? No longer feeling guilt for wrongs done or regrets for past failures and lost opportunities? No longer being influenced or forced to do wrong by authorities or suffering emotional pain inflicted by others? In the next life we can expect freedom and safety at last, a perfectly righteous world where all of us will live honorably all the time. "Wickedness will not rest upon the land of the righteous, so that the righteous will not put forth their hands to do wrong." We will live in a righteous realm where Jesus rules, not wickedness.

THE NEW EARTH

What does the Bible say about the future of our physical earth? I once heard a theology professor say that we think of heaven as being *up there* somewhere. But is it? Does the Bible actually teach us God's kingdom of heaven, or at least part of heaven, will be *down here* on a new or restored planet (Matthew 5:5; 6:10)? When Jesus comes and we raise from the dead, will we go *up to live forever in a distant heaven*, or will we be with Christ as our reigning king on a newly formed earth with access to a promised city existing somewhere within his realm (Hebrews 11:16; 13:14; Revelation 21:1-2)? The idea mentioned by the professor is that heaven, God's eternal kingdom, is not a distant place out in space somewhere, totally foreign to anything we have ever known; rather, it is a place somewhat familiar to us—*maybe* even including the same earth we now inhabit—restored, yet having other-worldly aspects. Can we say the Bible offers this possibility?

There is no question that God promises to create a new earth as our home. It is stated plainly in both the Old and New Testaments (Isaiah 65:17; 66:22; 2 Peter 3:13; Revelation 21:1).[15] One question is whether it will be this same earth, ruined (destroyed) on God's Day of Judgment but then renovated, or whether it will be a totally new earth, not the same one we now live on. Or, to add a second question, will there be more than one historical age for the future of the earth? When I read the Bible, I get the impression there will be a time when the present earth is ruled by Jesus and the saints for a lengthy period (a millennial age as in Isaiah 65:17-25). Then beyond that, there will be a new heaven and earth distinct from the previous one (as in Revelation 21:1-7). Whatever the answer to these questions, it is going to be fantastic, for who can think that any good world of God's making would be less satisfyingly beautiful and pleasing than this one? But are there any clues in the Bible to make us think the earth may be the same earth we now live in, remade and changed in significant ways from its present condition? Or that the earth will include a renovated history followed by a totally new history? The scriptures have been interpreted as seemingly contradictory. For example, how can the new earth of Isaiah 65 still have death of humans but the new earth in Revelation 21 have no death? Following are a few scriptures that give rise to the above-stated questions.

Romans 8:18-25 supports the idea of the earth being redeemed and renewed as mankind's continued home. In this passage we are told all creation, humans and the cosmos, are waiting to be set free from bondage to corruption. When humans fell and became separated from God, resulting in suffering and death, the earth and

15. The N.T. Greek word for *new* (*kainos*), used to describe the earth, is defined in *Vines Expository Dictionary of Old and New Testament Words*, Vol. 3 (New Jersey: Fleming H. Revel Company, Lo-Ser, 1981), 109, as "that which is unaccustomed or unused, not new in time, but new as to form or quality, of a different nature from what is contrasted as old."

nature also became corrupted (Genesis 3:17-19). God's plan is not only to redeem our human bodies but also to redeem his created earth. The earth suffers along with humans; mankind and nature are bound together. Paul treats the earth as a living thing; even our physical planet groans and suffers, waiting for humans to be redeemed so it too can be set free from its suffering. Our hope is that earth will enjoy a glorious future along with our bodies. This is expected to happen as a result of Jesus' next coming.

In Acts 3:19-21, the Apostle Peter preaches God's Word, saying that the Lord will "send Jesus, the Christ appointed for you, whom heaven must receive until the period of restoration of all things." Our earth had an original condition. "In the beginning, God created the heavens and the earth" and declared everything he made to be good (Genesis 1:1, 31). Obviously, it is no longer good since evil has spoiled it. To restore it is to remove the corruption and return it to a state of goodness, the difference being that, just like our resurrected bodies, the new goodness will include other-dimensional properties. Is that God's intention? Does the term *restoration* refer to a period of time when a string of many events takes place, including or leading up to a new earth?

Peter mentions new heavens and earth in a context of God's judgment when "the earth and its works will be burned up" (2 Peter 3:10-13). He likens it to the cleansing of the flood in Noah's day (2 Peter 3:3-7). Could it be that this is part of the earth's renovation—to be cleansed of wickedness by the judgment of fire before it is restored? The concept of earth being renovated fits in with Old Testament prophecies of new conditions found on a new earth (Isaiah 65:17-25). This promise as described in Isaiah implies what many believe to be a millennial age, a historical time period on earth when Christ and his people rule, when people live out their lives in peace and prosperity, when the wolf and the lamb will graze together. I know that most of Christendom is purported to believe in the eschatological (future things) view known as a-millennialism (no time period of Christ ruling on this present earth). But if the overall words of the totality of scripture are taken at face value, to my mind, there seems nothing to prevent the possibility of a millennial age.

Jesus seemed to imply such an age in comments he made to his disciples. On one occasion, Peter asked Jesus what the disciples would get for leaving all to follow him. Jesus said that in the *regeneration* (rebirth or renewing of world conditions), Jesus will sit on his throne, and the disciples will sit on thrones as judges of the tribes of Israel, whatever that might mean (Matthew 19:28). In Luke's account of the Last Supper, Jesus said that since his disciples shared in his trials, they would eat and drink in his kingdom and judge the tribes of Israel (Luke 22:28-30). I know these comments are taken by some to refer to what the disciples will do in the present church age before Jesus comes again, but still, one has to wonder if Jesus meant something more than that, especially in light of scriptures that speak of the saints ruling with Christ when he comes in his kingdom at the end of this age (Daniel 7:18, 21-22, 27; 1 Corinthians 6:2-3; 2 Timothy 2:12; Revelation 2:26-27; 3:21; 20:4-5).

There are a number of scriptures stating that the earth (or world) will wear out, pass away, perish, or be destroyed (Hebrews 1:10-12; Psalm 102:25-26; Isaiah 51:6; Matthew 5:18; 24:35; 2 Peter 3:10-13; 1 John 2:17; Revelation 21:1). Do these words mean the present earth is going out of existence, to be replaced by an entirely new earth? When the Bible says the earth is *passing away* or *will pass away* or will be *destroyed*, could it mean it is in process of coming to the end of its present condition then acquiring a new immortal condition, one that is eternal and cannot pass away, one that is beyond the conditions of death, which are still present in the millennial age? It is certainly possible that God does away with the heavens and earth altogether and creates new ones. But could it also be that the heavens and the earth will go through a similar transformation as Jesus' body and our bodies? They pass away, not going out of existence, not being replaced by something totally foreign to us, but being set free from corruption and possessing newness that exhibits both dissimilarity and sameness.

Some believe the following scripture is against the present earth being renovated. It says the earth and heaven fled away from God's presence and no place was found for them (Revelation 20:11). Taken for what it says, it appears to be an argument pointing to God as altogether done with this earth, requiring an entirely new earth to be created. This means that other scriptures having to do with the earth passing away or being destroyed would be understood to say, "be no more, perish, and come to an end of their existence." But is it possible that since the above verse is set in a context of God's judgment, it means that even the earth, because of all its corruption, is pictured as fleeing from such judgment, "knowing" it cannot exist in its present condition in the presence of a holy and righteous God? Or, could verses like this mean that the millennial age is over and the earth in a worn-out condition is changed (Hebrews 1:10-12; Psalm 102:25-26; Isaiah 51:6) and a new heaven and earth free of all death is created? Sorry to stop here, but it would take another book's worth or more to explore these questions in greater detail.

What is to be concluded from the Bible's view of earth history? Some say, according to the following verse, we will not know what the future earth is like, but whatever is coming will be wonderful beyond our imagination. The verse says, "Things which eye has not seen and ear has not heard, and have not entered the heart of man, all God has prepared for those who love him" (1 Corinthians 2:9-10). I agree, but the Bible does report there will be a new heaven and a new earth (Isaiah 65:17; 66:22; 2 Peter 3:13; Revelation 21:1). The hope that gives me great anticipated joy is that when I come into the next age, I will come to some sort of new and beautiful world having some degree of continuity to this one.

Can it be true? According to scriptures like Romans 8, yes it can. In fact, the more I become familiar with the Bible's overall story, the stronger is my suspicion that God is, initially at least, going to take back his earth and turn it into a heavenly place. To be sure, I have many unanswered questions having to do with a possible millennial age, and another age after that, and when and where and how everything will work, but I feel quite confident of one point at least: the invisible *soul stuff* of God's creation will not end up separated from the visible *physical stuff* of God's creation. New forms may take shape, but the new forms according to biblical promises will involve an evil-free continuation of good and beautiful things we are familiar with. Maybe I will not have to leave all of the beauty, wonder, and delight I have come to enjoy in this world. Who knows? God knows!

Many take comfort in the vision given by the Lord to the Apostle John. The vision reveals some of the differences that will be present in a future age of our world when all things will be made new (Revelation 21:5). There will be no more death, crying, pain, or evil of any kind. God will forevermore be present with us, and we will be his people. There will be a new city coming down to where we are; people from the earth are said to be going into it (Revelation 21:2, 23-27). This could be the city whose builder and maker is God, promised to Abraham and all who have faith like his (Hebrews 11:8-10; 13-16). A city implies we will maintain social relationships in familiar settings.

What did Jesus promise his followers when he was on earth? He promised that he would go ahead of us and prepare a place for us (John 14:2). It's OK that we may not all envision the same things about that place (Romans 14:22), but in the midst of this life's tribulations, afflictions, sufferings, and death, it is a comfort to be hoping and expecting God's promised glorious end. Though we are living in this present world, we belong to and are citizens of that new and yet-to-come world of God's making.

WORK IN THE NEXT LIFE

One morning, I glanced out a library window and noticed a woman across the street, tending to her beautiful flower garden. She seemed to be enjoying it. I thought about how much a part of life it is for us to work at various jobs and recreational hobbies. It seems we all have our individual interests in differing occupations and activities. I heard one parent saying to a child, "When you choose your life work, be sure it is something you enjoy doing." Work has an important function in God's design for a good life. God created a world of interdependence, meaning that all things depend on what they give to each other for their existence and well-being. We are beings who need each other, including our Creator. Work is how we serve and meet one another's needs. Work, which also involves times of recreation, is meant to give us great joy.

I could not live without family, farmers, food processors, truck drivers, those who make building materials, workers skilled in the trades, discoverers of medicines, scientists and inventors, teachers, health care providers, times of play, and on and on. On top of that, artistic people produce music, art, theater, and so forth, things that lift our souls in wonder and delight. There is every reason to be grateful for all good things. Work is meant to be pleasurable, fulfilling, and meaningful. God verified that he created us for work when he put us in charge of ruling, discovering, and maintaining this earth (Genesis 1:26-32; 2:5-8). Why would God limit work only to this earth when he intends for us to live on a new earth? Why will work not also be a meaningful part of the next world? Serving God and reigning with Jesus implies some form of work (Matthew 25:19-23; Revelation 5:10; 22:3, 5).

God is infinite, creative, a God of newness. Certainly there will never be an end of things to discover, learn, do, and enjoy. If God made us to be creative like him, why would we lose creativity in heaven? A promise in the Bible is that God will give us the desires of our heart (Psalm 37:4). I don't know what all that includes, but I do not think our desires involving the real work we would like to do are all fulfilled in this life. I love landscaping, making things beautiful. I have not had opportunity in this life to do it. I often wonder if God would give me one of those seemingly unused planets in space and say, "Go landscape it." Who knows? God knows, but I am confident there will be no boredom in the next world.

JESUS: OUR BLESSED HOPE

By being connected to Jesus, we have a blessed hope (Titus 2:13). I said at the beginning of this chapter that I am not down-playing the fact that above all I desire to be with God and my beloved Jesus and with loved ones. I am reminded of a statement made by D. A. Carson: "Fallen people like you and me readily fixate on God's gifts and ignore the Giver. At some point, this degenerates into worshiping the created thing rather than the Creator" (Romans 1:25).[16] Even though I want to be satisfied in my mind that our future body and the new earth will be similar to what we now know, and even though I feel personally satisfied by the Bible's revelations about them, I want to put emphasis on Jesus and his love for me, for it is his love that never fails, it is his love that makes life satisfying and enjoyable, and it

---

16. D. A. Carson, *For the Love of God*, Vol. 1, June 4 Meditation (Wheaton, IL: Crossway, June 4, 1998).

is his love that brings to us the future good things humans hope for. I hate it when I am self-centered, wrapped up in my own world, and uncaring toward God, Jesus, and others. More than anything else, I want my heart to be satisfied that when I meet Jesus, I will feel a true bond of love between us. Therefore, I want to emphasize putting Jesus and his love first in my life, for he embodies our blessed hope.

To those of us who have never seen him, as we grow in experiencing his love and as we grow to love him more and more (1 Peter 1:8-9), our most blessed hope is that one day we will be with the one who loved us more than anyone ever could. I realize he loves me when I experience answers to my prayers, when I remember my fear of dying and the peace he flooded into my soul the day I first believed, or when I notice how circumstances in my life must have been him at work to provide for my well-being, or when I look back and see how he has led my life and given me direction in times of confusion. I thank him for all of this. But I would have to say my deepest experience of his love was the time I first realized it was my sins and wrongs that put him on the cross. I broke down under feelings of deep sorrow and could not stop sobbing as I managed to get out these words: "I am so sorry, it was because of my sinfulness and wrong things I have done, and continue to do, that you had to go to the cross and suffer such an unbearable agony. I put you there, and I am deeply sorry." His forgiveness is one of the greatest experiences of love any human could have.

Another time, feeling particularly unworthy and wondering if anyone loved me, in all sincerity, and reaching out for affirmation, I asked him, "Do you love me?" I heard his gentle words in my mind: *Yes, I love you.* It was not just a mind-trip; he says the same in his written Word (1 John 4:16, 19). God delights in having us as his children, heirs of all he promises. When we are down, experiencing his love brings us back to life, awakens joy in us, and gives us courage to re-engage a tough world. When we who believe in Jesus meet him, I wonder if we will be able to meet him unashamedly (1 John 2:28), having full assurance of his love for us, and say we love him too. Or, will we be unable to look at him because we have loved *the things* he gave us rather than *the one* who gave his life for us (John 15:13; 10:10-16)? I have wondered that about myself and do not want that to happen. What greater hope could we have than the hope of enjoying an intimate friendship with Jesus and walking with him in uninterrupted unity?

I enjoy watching sporting events like football and basketball. I usually have a favorite team I root for, and when I watch a game I experience many different emotions. You can observe these emotions on the faces of individuals watching the game from the stands. During a game there are good things that happen and bad things that happen. When the game is going your way, you cheer and are happy. But when the game is going badly, you may experience anger, faultfinding, fears and doubts about the outcome, disappointment, or sadness and dejection. Sometimes I watch a replay of a game I missed, but I already know the final score. When I know how the game ends I don't go through all those up and down emotions; I am relaxed and enjoy the game. The bad things don't upset me because I know how the game ends.

Having Christian hope is to know the ending of life's ups and downs. Kyle Idleman, in his book on grace, has a chapter on being hopeful in times of despair. Knowing God's grace-filled promises in the midst of hard times changes our outlook. I really like his comment, "perhaps knowing how it will end allows us to not just endure the journey but actually to enjoy it."[17] Is that possible, to have joy in the midst of sufferings?

I don't know about you, but when I hope in something good that is coming, I am excited about it and I look forward to it, and when I think about it, such expectation gives me great joy. One thing that enabled Jesus to endure the agony of the cross was the joy that was set before him (Hebrews 12:2). What was that joy? It was seeing into the future and having the certainty that what he did on the cross would result in bringing many people to God and eternal life (Isaiah 53:4-6, 10-12). When going through hard times to endure afflictions, troubles, or persecutions, or simply facing death in the normal course of living, it is hope in Christ that becomes the anchor of our soul (Hebrews 6:17-19). The hope of entering more fully into the peaceful rest and joy of knowing Jesus and God the Father, possessing a new body, enjoying life on a new earth, and being part of a well-ordered society made up of God's people enables us to endure all the hardships that we may face. We can say with certainty that what

---

17. Kyle Idleman, *Grace Is Greater* (Grand Rapids, MI: Baker Books, 2017), 174.

happens to us in this life matters very little compared to the fantastic future awaiting us (Romans 8:18).

I've always loved fairy-tales. They take you to enchanting and magical lands where wonderful things happen and life is lived happily ever after. Why do people like fairy-tales? I'm inclined to think that people write them and tell them and make movies of them because this art form is a reflection of how people wish their lives really were. Some think the Bible, with all its miracles, is a fairy-tale, and when you think about it, it really does sound very much like a fairy-tale. It is sometimes hard to believe, but unlike the wishful thinking in our made-up fairy-tales that we wish would come true, we have valid reason to believe the Bible is true and that the things written that have been promised by a faithful God will come to pass (Revelation 22:6-7).

When I have doubts about my faith and wonder if all these hopes are really true and worth believing in, I ask myself, *Did Jesus Christ really live, die, and rise again from the dead?* Because if he did, that settles the issue for me—and for many others.[18] When I doubt, I review what I know about the historical records and am convinced all over again that Jesus was a real person in our history and that eyewitnesses passed on to us true information about his life, death, and resurrection. The reputable eyewitnessed resurrection of the body of our Lord Jesus Christ is evidence of the truth of my faith (John 20:28-29).[19] But of greater evidence still, beyond evidences for Jesus' life, death, and resurrection and evidences in biblical testimonies, is the very real personal experience and relationship I enjoy with him. Knowing he indwells my life is my assurance that eternal life in God's future kingdom, including a new heaven and earth, is real (2 Corinthians 13:5; Colossians 1:24-27; 1 John 5:11-12). If we are following the Lord Jesus Christ, he will take us there and complete our hope of glory (John 10:27-28; 14:1-3).

---

18. Antony Flew, *There Is a God: How the world's most notorious atheist changed his mind* (New York: Harper One, 2007). In this book, one of the things that helped the author believe in God was N. T. Wright's argument for the resurrection of Jesus, the basic points of which he includes in Appendix B, "What Evidence is There for the Resurrection of Jesus?" 195-213.

19. W. Mark Lanier, *Christianity on Trial: A lawyer examines the Christian faith* (Downers Grove, IL: InterVarsity Press, 2014), 186-210. The author, a well-known and respected trial lawyer, explains how witnesses are chosen for the courtroom, what makes a valid witness, and shows why the witnesses of Jesus' resurrection are reliable.

CHAPTER 7

FACING GOD'S JUDGMENTS WITH HOPE

We can't deal with the subject of hope and what the world is coming to without discussing the judgment of God, for it too is coming. God clearly warns, "Therefore having overlooked the times of ignorance, God is now declaring to men that all people everywhere should repent, because He has fixed a day in which He will judge the world in righteousness through a Man whom He has appointed, having furnished proof to all men by raising Him from the dead" (Acts 17:30-31; see also Matthew 16:26-27; Revelation 22:12). In this chapter we shall consider the nature of a loving God and why he must be a God of judgment. We shall briefly review various judgments of God mentioned in scripture and look at biblical truths that help those who fear facing God's judgment. Finally, we will deal with the problem of self-judgment and self-condemnation.

The Bible clearly portrays the judgment and justice aspect of God's nature. For example:

- "And there is no creature hidden from His sight, but all things are open and laid bare to the eyes of Him with whom we have to do" (Hebrews 4:13).

- "For God will bring every act to judgment, everything which is hidden, whether it is good or evil" (Ecclesiastes 12:14; see also 3:16-17).

- "For He is coming to judge the earth. He will judge the world in righteousness and the peoples in His faithfulness" (Psalm 96:13).

- "For it is time for judgment to begin with the household of God; and if it begins with us first, what will be the outcome for those who do not obey the gospel of God?" (1 Peter 4:17).

- "It is appointed for men to die once and after this comes judgment" (Hebrews 9:27).

How shall we respond to these warnings of coming judgment? You may say, "I don't believe any of that stuff. This is not a God I want to believe in." I can respect that, and you can believe what you want. But what if there is a God of judgment and justice? Rather than deny or ignore it, would it not be wise to think about the possibility and learn what it takes to be prepared to meet him? (2 Peter 3:11-14; 1 John 3:2-3).

THE NATURE OF A LOVING GOD AND WHY HE MUST BE A GOD OF JUDGMENT

God's judgment is a subject seldom thought about or talked about. This is understandable, for the idea frightens people, or it should (Psalm 24:3-4; Matthew 7:21-23; 2 Corinthians 5:10; Hebrews 10:26-27, 30-31). People prefer to believe in a God of love because anger, wrath, and judgment seem out of character for a loving God. It would seem so, and God is love (1 John 4:8). God is compassionate, merciful, and forgiving, but he will not leave the wrongdoer unpunished (Exodus 34:6-7). Because evil destroys love, love must exercise judgment and justice.

One evening, in our small town, there was a shooting. A stranger was randomly shooting at people and had already killed one person and wounded another. A man drove into the area to pick up his wife from work and saw what was happening. He took a rifle from his pick-up and shot at the sniper, chasing him away. The whole town was in lock-down until the gunman was apprehended by police. At the time, my wife and I were at a high school basketball game and could not leave the school until word came that it was safe. The town and county's system of law and order was thrust into action until the situation was under control and the town was restored to a safe place for its citizens.

We must not forget that law and order is a God-ordained function of good government (Romans 13:1-5). Without it, society is chaotic at best and evil at worst. However, law and order cannot exist without citizens who are willing to live by a justice system that deals with violators. If the bad guys get away with crimes against law-abiding citizens, it is not good, and it is not right. Love and justice cannot allow it. Whether those crimes are outward acts of physical violence or unnoticed acts of cheating people through dishonesty, law and order is needed to protect people from evils that disrupt or destroy their lives.

Judgment inflicts deserved punishments designed to curb illegal activities so people can live safely and securely. Like humanity's need for law and order, God's judgment is also a system of law and order, designed to sustain what is good and eliminate what is evil. Ultimately, God's judgment will be instrumental in creating a renewed world of righteousness (Psalm 9:7-8; 96:11-13). Judgment and justice are necessary in a world like ours where evil often triumphs. I think it odd that we accept society's necessary practice of judgment and justice, but when it comes to God, we deny him the right to do the same. In fact, without full knowledge of God's true nature and the circumstances surrounding his judgments, we criticize him as mean and unloving or we dispense with such a God altogether.[20]

Why must God judge? If God is holy and righteous, he would be guilty of injustice by allowing wrongdoing and crimes against the

---

20. I recognize this is a difficult subject for many people, including myself. We might be helped in our attitude toward God if more study and writings were done on this topic and if more people were interested enough to read them. For a helpful read on the anger and judgment of God, try John Mark Comer, *God Has a Name* (Grand Rapids, MI: Zondervan, 2017), 155-187. Another helpful read is Paul Copan, *Is God a Moral Monster: Making Sense of the Old Testament God* (Grand Rapids, MI: Baker Books, 2011).

innocent to go unpunished. We humans have a moral sense about us that life is very unfair if wrong is not made right. We especially think this when the wrongs are done to us. Here are three examples of situations in which we welcome a God of judgment to intervene on our behalf.

1. A man who adamantly believed in a God of love and refused to believe in a God of judgment changed his mind when his wife was raped and brutally murdered. Out of deepest grief and all-consuming anger, he came to believe that if God is not a God of judgment, he would not be worth worshiping.

2. Souls who have been martyred for their faith cry out to God, "How long, O Lord, holy and true, will You refrain from judging and avenging our blood on those who dwell on the earth?" (Revelation 6:9-10). It is only just for God to repay with affliction those who afflict the innocent (2 Thessalonians 1:6-8).

3. I once was very angry toward unknown persons who vandalized my property. I lost sleep planning ways to get even. One night, God reminded me of a Bible verse that said not to take revenge but to let him bring about justice in his time (Romans 12:19). Even though justice was not happening now, knowing that God intends to right all wrongs enabled me to let go of my angry resentments and bitterness, to forgive, and to grow in love (a willingness to do good) toward those I once hated.

We may not understand or like a God of judgment, but the fact that people criticize God if he does nothing about the evils in the world shows they believe in the necessity and rightness of judgment.

It may be difficult to understand that judgment and appropriate punishment issues forth from God's love. But we understand this on a human level. Suppose a child disobeys a parent by dashing out into the street. The driver of a car puts on the brakes as the parent is pulling the child to safety. At that moment the parent is having two emotions. On the one hand, the parent is relieved and grateful that the child is all right and may hug the child. But at the same time, the parent is angry and punishes the child for disobedience in hopes that the punishment will be painful enough to prevent the child from doing it again. The parent's anger and judgment of wrongdoing and the issuing of a consequence come out of love and concern for the child.

God's judgment is sometimes like that—an act of love to help a person make a needed correction or life change. At other times, God's judgment is an act of love when he separates people from society who are harming others and who have no intention of stopping. He does so to protect the innocent from evil. A God of judgment is welcomed by good people when they are guaranteed an evil-free world (Proverbs 11:10). Of course, none of us likes to be personally judged, but not liking it does not mean it is unnecessary. God's judgment comes only out of necessity, and God knows when it is time. But whether immediate or future, it is rarely, if ever, without love-motivated warnings, giving time for persons to change and avoid it. The truth is, God is love and does not want anyone to perish (Ezekiel 18:23, 32; John 3:16; 2 Peter 3:9).

PAST- AND PRESENT-DAY JUDGMENTS OF GOD

HISTORICAL ACTS OF GOD

In God's history book we learn of many judgments in this life. The flood in Noah's day was a judgment on the wicked for their fixed mindset of unrepentant violence (Genesis 6:13). God brought a judgment of plagues on the Egyptians for afflicting the Israelites so he could deliver them from their captors (Genesis 15:13-14). God destroyed Sodom and Gomorrah by fire for their sinfulness (Genesis 19:13, 24-25). God sent famine for the sin of Saul (2 Samuel 21:1). God judged his own people, Israel, for idolatry and their failure to acknowledge God as the only life-giving God (2 Kings 17:14-20; Jeremiah 5:3; 8:5-6). God threatened destruction to Nineveh for its evils (Jonah 1:1-2; 3:10). God put Ananias and Sapphira to death for lying to him (Acts 5:1-11). These past judgments of God have been recorded and serve as warnings to help people realize the danger to themselves of repeating the same wrongs (1 Corinthians 10:6-11; 2 Peter 2:6).

It is reasonable to believe, based on God's recorded history, that some events in our present day are likely to be judgments of God. When the Twin Towers in New York City were destroyed by airplanes crashing into them, it was said publicly by some that this was a judgment by God on our nation. Those who said this were quickly reprimanded publicly for saying such a thing, largely in deference to the victims and their hurting families. In today's world it is not politically correct or popular to say such things. It cannot be said that every natural disaster or bad thing that happens is a judgment of God for a particular evil, but Jesus did imply that disasters can serve as warnings of a need for repentance lest we become subject to similar calamities (Luke 13:1-5).

Scriptures also say that God is consistent with his Word, and even though he warns of coming judgment, in his love, mercy, and grace, he will not bring judgment if repentance and faith are exercised (Exodus 34:6-7; Jeremiah 18:7-10; Jonah 3:10-4:2). He is patient and gives warnings and time for people to repent and change. For example, he waited over four hundred years for the Amorites to come to a place of deserved judgment (Genesis 15:12-16; Leviticus 18:24-25; Joshua 24:11; Amos 2:9-10).

NATURAL CONSEQUENCES OF PROLONGED WRONGDOING

For some who refuse to give up their destructive and sinful ways, God's judgment is to let them go their way and let their own sinful habits be their judgment (Numbers 32:23; Jeremiah 2:19; Romans 1:28-32). Sometimes, seeing the destructiveness of what our sinful life is doing to us can lead us to give up the ways we are living and seek a new way of life (Ephesians 2:1-5).

DISCIPLINING BELIEVERS

The Apostle Paul points out that God sometimes sends disciplinary judgments on believers to correct their wrongs and protect them from being condemned along with the world. God's discipline comes from his love so that we may grow into the likeness of our Lord and share in his holiness (Hebrews 12:5-29). These disciplines are not to condemn us but to help us. We receive

104

them with thanksgiving and allow ourselves to be trained by them, even though they are painful at the time.

Regarding such measures, the Apostle Paul tells us in a letter to the Corinthian church how we can avoid God's disciplinary judgments, that we can do it by exercising self-judgment (1 Corinthians 11:27-31). In the context of this scripture, he says there are two areas of self-judgment of particular concern. We are to make sure we are in harmony with Jesus' character and teachings and also in harmony with our fellow Christians. If we faithfully judge ourselves, we won't need the judgment and discipline of God that comes because of failure to acknowledge and correct our wrongs. Therefore, if we judge ourselves, we will not be judged. This self-judgment is practiced when we promptly admit we are wrong, receive God's forgiveness, move on without guilt or self-condemnation, and continue to do what's good and right.

REJECTING GOD'S JUDGMENT ON OUR BEHALF

Jesus did not come to judge and condemn you for your sins; he came to be judged for your sins (John 12:47; 1 Peter 2:24). God judged our sin at the cross of Jesus by pouring out his just wrath upon his Son as payment for your sins and mine (Isaiah 53:4-8; Romans 8:3). "He Himself bore our sins in His own body on the cross," and the Father judged his Son by putting him to death (1 Peter 2:24). This was God's love: he himself suffering that which we all deserve (Romans 5:6-8). If we reject the sin-bearer, the one who paid for our sins, then what condemns us is rejecting the one whose love made possible our forgiveness and reconciliation to God (John 3:16-18; Romans 5:10-11).

THE BIBLE AS JUDGE

God also judges us in everyday life through his written Word. God's Word judges us when we read it. It tells us our present condition, correcting our twisted or harmful thinking to help us change wrong behaviors. It exposes our inner thoughts and desires (Psalm 119:75-77; Hebrews 4:12-13). Jesus said that those who have heard his words and have rejected him will be judged by his words on the last day (John 12:48).

END-OF-THE-WORLD JUDGMENTS OF GOD

THE DAY OF THE LORD

This phrase, *the Day of the Lord*, is frequently used in the Old and New Testaments to describe God's judgment upon an ungodly world (Isaiah 13:6-13; Acts 17:30-31). It is a day of reckoning against all the proud (Isaiah 2:12, 17-22). It will be a day of destruction, darkness, and gloom (Joel 1:15; 2:1-2, 11-13; Amos 5:18-20). Toward the end of the world as we know it, people of the world will be saying, "peace and safety," thinking everything is all right. But there is no peace and safety because the Day of Judgment will suddenly come (1 Thessalonians 5:2-10; see also Jeremiah 6:14; Ezekiel 13:10). It is the day of cleansing and the establishment of a new earth (Romans 8:19-21; 2 Peter 3:10-13). God's people will be rescued just before this day begins (1 Thessalonians 1:9-10; 5:9), then God's wrathful judgments and woes described in Revelation will begin (Revelation 6:12-17; chapters 7–10, 16).

There is hope for escape if repentance occurs (Joel 2:31-32). But beware; God knows the difference between those who repent only to save their lives and those whose repentance is genuine (2 Corinthians 7:10). In the very last days, God's judgments will bring cursing from men rather than repentance (Revelation 16:1-11). It is this refusal to never repent and accept God's offer of salvation that seals our separation from God (Deuteronomy 18:18-19; John 3:36; Romans 2:5).

Does God want to see people judged and put to death? Jesus said that he came first to save the world, not to judge it (John 12:47). It is clear that God does not desire the death of anyone but that all come to repentance and be saved from pending wrath (Ezekiel 18:30-32; 2 Peter 3:9). But after God's many merciful warnings and our refusal to heed them, the Lord's Day of Judgment will finally come.

THE GREAT WHITE THRONE JUDGMENT

In Revelation 20:11-15, the Great White Throne Judgment separates the ungodly from the righteous; the evil from the good; the unbeliever and fake believer from the true believer. The result of this judgment determines our final destination in eternity (John 5:24, 28-29;

2 Peter 3:7). This judgment also results in the existence of a new and evil-free world (John 5:24, 28-29; 2 Peter 3:7, 13; Revelation 21:1-5). The Bible guarantees God's judging of every person's deeds, good and bad (Matthew 10:26-28; 12:36-37; 16:27; Ecclesiastes 12:14). Unbelievers will be judged during the White Throne Judgment, and although they cannot expect entrance into God's kingdom because of their refusal to want God to reign over them, perhaps God's judgment of their deeds will help decide a degree of severity that will be experienced by them in their next world (Matthew 11:20-24).

I remember a nightmare I had as a teen in which I actually died and went to hell. The terrible things I remember were lifeless barrenness and the torturous thought of being confined there forevermore. Hans Schwarz stated that phrases like a "weeping and gnashing of teeth" (Matthew 22:13) "express the anguish of knowing what one has missed without the possibility of ever reaching it. They witness to a state of extreme despair without the hope of reversing it."[21] Some say being cast away from God forever is unfair, too great a punishment for the limited amount of time on earth and the few sins we've committed compared to all our goodness. Does the Bible teach that people are cast into hell because of their sins, or is it for their unrelenting refusal to repent and be on God's side (Romans 2:1-11)? How can anyone live peaceably and happily with God when they do not want to be there?[22]

THE JUDGMENT SEAT OF CHRIST

The Judgment Seat of Christ (2 Corinthians 5:10; Romans 14:10-12) is for believers and has nothing to do with condemnation for our sins or determining our salvation. That was settled at the cross of Christ (Romans 3:21-26). Seemingly, this judgment is to determine rewards for how we have served God and Christ with our lives (1 Corinthians 3:8-15). In a parable Jesus told about the master who comes back to judge how his servants did with what he gave them (Luke 19:11-27), there is positive reward for the productive work of believers, but those who did not do the

---

21. Hans Schwarz, *Eschatology* (Eerdmans: Grand Rapids, MI, 2000), 402.

22. I dealt extensively with this subject in my book *Out of Darkness into the Light*, chapter 10, "Does God send good people to hell?"

works God gifted them to do will lose their reward. People usually equate judgment only with evils and punishment, but God's judgment is also one of commendation. He will judge the good we do, and his rewards and commendations will be richly celebrated and enjoyed. Jesus said that even a cup of cold water given to a person in need will be rewarded (Proverbs 25:21-22; Matthew 10:42). It is very encouraging to think that Jesus will be greatly pleased with much that we have done in his name (Matthew 5:2-11; 25:21, 23; 1 Corinthians 15:58; Ephesians 6:7-8). However, scripture does indicate that when Jesus comes, believers who have not done the good works God created us for have the possibility of shrinking or cowering before him in shame (Ephesians 2:10; Titus 2:11-14; 1 John 2:28).

Some believe emphasis on rewards is a bad thing because we should not be working for rewards but to humbly obey what Jesus calls us to do out of love for him. True enough; we do serve out of love and not for rewards. Personally, in all my years as a follower of Christ, I have given little or no thought to rewards. I simply try and live my life the best I can, obey God's Word the best I can, and if I am striving to mature in Christ Jesus and am willingly involved in his good works, I have no cause to fear his judgment or loss. What a wonderful commendation it is to hear from God, "Well done, good and faithful servant." We all fail in areas of serving Jesus, but we all do good things too, and those good things will be rewarded.

Others believe rewards are bad because they will create jealousy or rivalry on earth and in heaven. Absolutely not! This thought can serve as a caution for church people on earth, but in heaven there is no evil thinking or competition to get ahead of others, only enjoyment of life in a new world free of evil. God is good, and his true kingdom on earth consists of righteousness, peace, and joy in serving Christ (Romans 14:17-19).

THE JUDGMENT OF ANGELS

Amazingly, Christians are said to be a judge of angels. It is also said that we will judge the world (1 Corinthians 6:2-3). Satan's judgment began at the cross of Jesus (Genesis 3:15; Hebrews 2:14-15; 1 John 3:8) and will be completed when he is no longer allowed access to the new world (Matthew 25:41; Revelation 20:10).

THE JUDGMENT OF NATIONS

I am reminded of Mark Twain's statement, "It ain't the parts of the Bible that I can't understand that bother me, it's the parts that I do understand." The judgment of nations (Matthew 25:31-46) is one of the difficult parts of the Bible to understand, and Bible scholars offer a wide variety of interpretations for what this might mean. Bible scholars do give lots of helpful insights, but there yet remain unresolved questions to answer. I will give you some key questions about the text that you can work on if you wish.

1. What is the context of the story? Does it have any relationship to nations mentioned in Revelation 21:22-27?

2. What is meant by "all the nations"? Are they nations or individuals within nations? Who are they?

3. Who are "these brothers of Mine" and "the least of these"? They are not the ones being judged but are the recipients of good or ill treatment from the sheep and the goats.

4. Who are the sheep and the goats?

5. When and where does this event take place? Does it have anything to do with a millennial age on the earth (Isaiah 2:2-4) or not?

Since I am still seeking a satisfying explanation, I will be content to be bothered by the part of the Bible I do understand. Jesus identifies with people who are in need and cares about how we treat them. He requires us to minister to their basic needs (Matthew 25:37-40). It is so important to him that our ultimate destination is affected by it. Here is a warning to all Christians: faith without works is dead (James 2:17), and many who claim to be Christians may not be. Evidence of true faith in Jesus is to be involved in his works (Matthew 7:21-27).

OVERCOMING FEAR OF FACING GOD IN JUDGMENT

How do we face God's judgment for our sins? No one can stand uncondemned before a holy God (1 Samuel 6:20; Psalm 130:3; 143:2; Malachi 3:2; Romans 3:23). Can a murderer stand not guilty before a judge? Can a boy who breaks a neighbor's window stand not guilty before the neighbor? In each case, a penalty must be paid; the wrong must be righted. I don't know about you, but even as a believer in Christ Jesus, keen awareness of my failures has, at times, tempted me to feel uncertain in terms of where I stand with God. Even though there is a lot of good in my life, when I am honest, I know that I fall short in many areas. I feel I can always do more for God and am not doing all I should. Sometimes I have been tempted to think that I must not be a true Christian because of my selfishness and lack of selfless motivation.

There are a few times when I have wondered, *What does God think of me, and how will I face him in judgment?* When I realize my deep sinfulness and ungodliness that is totally unacceptable to a holy God, I can understand the terror that Martin Luther felt as he contemplated God's anger at sin. He was horrified at the thought of a wrathful God who judges his sin-filled life. That must be why many people choose not to think about the subject. Others justify themselves as being good with nothing to worry about, and some relieve themselves from all such worries by not believing in God. But if God's judgment is certain, what you or I choose to believe will never make facing him go away. How can I face a holy God without fear?

I search the scriptures to find any word of assurance and comfort that enables me to be free of fear. There I discover that the ultimate answer for being at peace in the face of God's judgment must be found in personally experiencing God's mercy and grace. This is extended to every one of us through faith in what Jesus did on the cross. Someone put it this way: God as our judge demonstrated his love for us by coming down to suffer the punishment for our sins so he could forgive us (Romans 5:8-9; 1 Timothy 2:3-5). If we have a hard time thinking God can forgive us for what we have done, we need to see and believe that Jesus, as a result of his sinless human life and voluntary sufferings, is now a qualified high priest who successfully intercedes with God on our behalf (Isaiah 53:12; Hebrews 7:24-27). If we grasp the truth of Christ's payment for our sin and of his continual intercession for us (1 John 2:1-2), then God's grace sinks into our heart and soul, and we have confidence that we shall live and not die; that we shall be lovingly accepted into his presence (Hebrews 4:14-16).

Faith must understand Jesus' death and how it frees us from our sin (Romans 6:4-7). Faith must believe that God remembers our sin no more (Psalm 103:11-14; Isaiah 43:25; Hebrews 8:12; 10:17). God takes pleasure in those who do not shrink back from believing his forgiveness. Confidence in the face of judgment can never be in oneself or in our good performances. No! In humble gratitude, we must rely totally and without reservation on the merits of our Great High Priest (Hebrews 10:19-23). Knowing his love for us replaces any fear of punishment or judgment. God desires a loving relationship with us, and this relationship of love casts out all fear (1 John 4:15-19).

God does not reveal the judgment side of his nature to scare us into yielding to him. He knows a forced yielding is no yielding at all. His love motivates us to love him in return. For my part, I seek to remain in God's love (Jude 20-21) through faith, meditation, prayer, ongoing repentance, obedience, fellowship, and by learning to love and meet needs as Jesus loves and meets needs. Seeing that I am growing in these areas by God's grace assures me that I do have a loving relationship with him. When I see God's answer to my fears, I humbly say, "Thank you, heavenly Father, for sending Jesus and for your unfathomable mercy and grace. I believe your Word that tells me, 'Therefore there is now no condemnation for those who are in Christ Jesus'" (Romans 8:1).

Dealing with Self-Judgment

One day a traveling homeless man stopped by my place, seeking money for food to help him along his way. He had a six pack of beer, and when I questioned his use of any money I might give him, to convince me he was not going to use the money for drinking, he took me to the curb and poured out every can of beer onto the street. Through his willingness to engage me in further conversation, I learned that he was running away from a good home where he had been living. A family had kindly taken him in, treated him as part of the family, and was helping him in every way they could. They loved and accepted him. I asked, "Why would you leave a caring home to live like this?" I learned he hated himself because he had destroyed his life and past relationships through drinking. He ran away from this family because he did not deserve their love, and he feared hurting them by failing them. I did help him on his way, but he needed to realize he was running from the very thing that would save him—love, acceptance, and God's help. He was running away because he judged himself as unworthy of being loved.

Sometimes we can be our own worst enemy; we are harder on ourselves than God is. He offers compassionate mercy, love, and acceptance, but we judge ourselves to the point of self-loathing and self-hatred. This is understandable when we look at awful things we have done or are doing and at the destructive results we are bringing on ourselves and others. It is easy to think we do not deserve goodness and love but only judgment and punishment. Self-judgment can happen when we listen to our own voice condemning us for our imperfections and failures. But self-judgment can also come when we listen to the voices of others—that is, people's criticisms, people's lifestyles when compared to our own, and Satan's accusations.

The Apostle Paul, in dealing with criticisms from others, writes that no one is qualified to sit in condemning judgment of another person's work or life and that I am not even to pronounce such judgment upon myself. He said that God is our ultimate judge, and two factors are necessary in order to judge accurately. We must have all the facts in the case, and we must know the motives involved. Without these at hand, it is arrogant for anyone to judge or criticize another (1 Corinthians 4:3-5).

The most accurate judge of anyone's life is God, for he knows us perfectly; therefore, we must accept his view of us. I defer my ultimate judgment to God, and I do not fear it because of Jesus' intercession on my behalf (1 John 2:1-2). When I humbly receive the forgiveness of God for my failures and imperfections, I can accept myself as imperfect because God accepts me. And if I have wronged others and given them reason to criticize me, I seek to regain their trust and forgiveness by making things right with them. If they forgive me, it helps my self-acceptance, but if not, I know I have done my part.

This does not mean we do not need to listen to others' criticisms. There is definitely benefit in hearing and heeding what others have to say (Proverbs 15:31-32), but actually, only God in Christ can perfectly judge. What this tells me is that I need to disregard my feelings of self-judgment based on criticisms and instead focus on forgiveness in Christ and on loving and serving God as genuinely as I can.

Not only does self-judgment come when we listen to the criticisms of others, but we can think ourselves unworthy or inferior when we compare ourselves with others. This has proved to be a problem when people compare themselves to others. When comparing themselves to people's perfectly portrayed images, others seem to have life so much better than they do. When we see that others look better or can do things better than us, we are apt to feel envious and think less of ourselves. Consider 1 Corinthians 12:14-25. It speaks about the parts of Christ's body, the church. When reading this we learn that each part of the body of Christ has a role to fill. I am not to look at others and think I need to be like them. I am to appreciate others and build them up. I am also to realize how God has gifted me and am responsible to fulfill my own part. Does the eye condemn itself because it does not do what the foot is doing? No, it does its own part in the body. If each does its own part, the whole body functions well.

Seeing God's acceptance of me, who he gifted me to be, and how pleased he is when I do my part the best I can helps me avoid thinking I am inferior or a failure by comparing myself to others. I need to focus on being myself, being grateful to God for his acceptance and the gifts he has given me, living my life the best I can according to God's will and design for me, and stop feeling like less of a person by comparing myself to others.

Self-judgment also comes when we believe the accusations of Satan. He will aim at our weaknesses, sins, and imperfections and tell us, "You are not a good Christian or person. Look at how you fail to live as God wants." Satan can speak these things not only into our minds but also through other people. We could easily believe the accusations because we do fail God and we know that we could be a godlier person.

In Revelation 12:10-11 we learn that we overcome Satan's accusations by the blood of the lamb and by our testimony. I take this to mean that when satanic thoughts come into our mind, we testify to our faith by saying, "You are right, I do not live all the time the way God wants me to live. But I confess those things to God, and because of what Jesus did for me on the cross, I am forgiven (1 John 1:9). I also realize my need to work on certain areas of my life. So be gone! You have no power to destroy my life. I believe in Jesus, and he is saving me." When we get off track and then get back on track of doing our best to live as God directs, we know we truly belong to God and do not have to fear the evil one's accusations. We have this same confidence when we see ourselves being faithful to Jesus if people poke fun at us or if they threaten us with harm—and even death.

A Practical Exercise to Increase Your Hope in Troublesome Times

People have a lot of fear about what's happening in our world today. There is a growing feeling that the world is increasingly becoming unsafe. To listen to the news media is depressing; the world seems to be spinning out of control. People are losing heart, becoming more and more stressed, and suffering increased anxieties, depression, and even despair. People are scared of the divisiveness and growing instability in their own country, fearful of where it is heading. People are scared their country might be taken over by terrorists or enemies with differing ideologies. People are scared of economic conditions, afraid of losing their money or their ability to meet their needs for survival. Environmental reports make thoughts of a possible end of our planet a growing concern. There is a lot to fear in the world, and hope is waning. What will happen to us? How can I have hope that renews in me a spirit of life and peace and joy?

As Christians, rather than fear violence, evil world conditions, and sufferings, we need to focus on God's perspective. If you are going through fearful circumstances or having fears of what is to come, plan times alone with God to let his Word speak hope into your troubled heart and mind. Feelings of hopelessness may arise within us, but we can work through them when we see God's plans and hear his encouraging words to not be afraid but to fill our thoughts with his life-giving words of hope.

There are many Bible passages that can be read, but I recommend beginning with these chapters: Isaiah 24, 25, 26; Psalms 37, 46, 47, 48, 49, 50, 73, and Romans 8. Sit in quietness before God, and ask him to bring a word especially meant to comfort and revive you, to give you courage to trust your life into his hands, and to receive his direction in the ways he would have you to go. Draw near to God, and let him cause hope to come to life in your heart—a life-giving hope in the midst of troublesome times.

To close this book on hope, I remind all of us that the Apostle Paul was well acquainted with troublesome times and suffering (2 Corinthians 11:23-28). Hope sustained him (2 Corinthians 4:7-18). His parting prayer for us is this: "And now may the God of hope fill you with all joy and peace in believing, so that you will abound in hope by the power of the Holy Spirit" (Romans 15:13).

APPENDIX:
THE VALUE OF SUFFERING[23]

Every human will experience some degree of suffering. Suffering is caused by evils that can be put into three classifications.

1. The first includes natural evils, the result of the corruption of nature (Genesis 3:17-18; 5:29; Romans 8:20-21) such as tornados, hurricanes, floods, famines, earthquakes, fires, and diseases.

2. The second is moral evils that result from the corruption of human nature (Matthew 15:19; Romans 3:23; Galatians 5:19-21; 2 Timothy 3:1-5; Hebrews 11:36-37). They include such things as lying, stealing, hating, murder, sexual abuse, verbal abuse, racism, wars, failure to love, disrespect for authority, persecutions, fears, guilt, depression, breakdowns in communication and relationships, and so forth. We humans cause much of our own suffering (Genesis 6:11-13).

3. A third classification includes supernatural evils that are a result of the acts of supernatural beings (Job 1–2; Mark 1:12-13; Luke 8:1–2; John 8:44). They include demonic possession, witchcraft, satanic temptations, acts of satanic power, and evil "rained upon us" by the judgments or acts of God, though always with a righteous purpose (Judges 9:23-24; 1 Samuel 16:14; 1 Kings 22:23; 2 Kings 6:33). Death is a consequence of evil (Romans 6:23).

---

23. Author's Note: Troublesome times means various degrees of suffering. In case you did not get this message in the book's introduction I will mention again that I felt the book needed a chapter on the subject of suffering to help readers see how God is able to use our sufferings for good. Rather than write another chapter, I decided to include, as an appendix, something I have already written. The content within this appendix is taken from chapter 15, "The Value of Suffering," from my previously published book, *Out of Darkness Into the Light, Learning to See Life from God's Point of View* (Bloomington, IN: Westbow Press, 2014).

Evil is a horrendous problem. Every culture, religion, philosophy, and individual must deal with it; we try to find an answer to it or ignore it. The existence of evil is a big reason some choose not to believe in God, and from their viewpoint, such a choice is understandable. How can there be an all-powerful, good, and loving God when these evils exist and cause such unthinkable sufferings? We will do all we humanly can to alleviate the suffering of our loved ones and others, but a supposed almighty, loving God remains silent and absent and does nothing. We could never let ourselves be like that and stand by and do nothing. Either such a God does not exist, has left us on our own, or does not care. Such a viewpoint is understandable. People having a hard time understanding why anyone would not believe in God have perhaps not seriously experienced or dealt with the magnitude of evil and suffering. Suffering is not easy to accept. Many confessing Christians have been angry with God in the midst of evil and have found themselves questioning and being tempted to disbelieve. Suffering has caused some to fall away from faith in God. We can easily ask, *Why isn't God helping us?*

All kinds of answers, called theodicies, have been proposed to justify God in the face of evil; some are better than others, and although God allows suffering to continue, he promises the ultimate answer—a time of judgment when all wrongs will be righted, all evil will be eliminated, and a new world will be brought into existence. God does not say why evil was allowed to exist in the first place, but it's here, and God assures us that those born of God, many having suffered unjustly, will live again in resurrected bodies and enjoy his righteous world forever. God is all-powerful, good, and loving and will prevent and destroy evil—but not yet (Acts 3:19-21; 17:31; 2 Corinthians 5:10; 2 Peter 3:7–14).

I agree with the theodicy that says that in an imperfect world like ours, it is possible that God has a good and sufficient reason for allowing evil to continue. Viktor Frankl, a noted Austrian psychiatrist, witnessed and experienced extreme inhumane treatment in four concentration camps. His pregnant wife, his parents, and his brother were all murdered. He said he was able to endure the horrendous sufferings by believing that meaning could be found even in suffering.[24] Could it be that one reason for God allowing evil to exist is that, for warranted reason, we need the opportunity to experience the value of suffering?

Jesus makes it clear that even in the face of suffering, God cares about us. Jesus was an exact representation of his Father (John 14:8–9; Hebrews 1:2–3). What Jesus said and did shows us God as he really is. Since Jesus had compassion on people who were suffering, he showed us by his many acts of kindness, healings, and feeding the poor that God cares about us (Matthew 9:35-36; 15:32-38; Mark 1:40-42). Even in the Old Testament, where God is sometimes unjustly criticized as being vindictive, angry, and condemning, it says he is compassionate (Exodus 34:5-6; Deuteronomy 4:31; Lamentations 3:21-24; Jonah 4:2). Peter agreed that God cares by telling us to "Give all your worries and cares to God, for he cares about you" (1 Peter 5:7-10). Admittedly, it is hard to accept that God cares if he seems not to be helping us in our sufferings, does not answer our prayers, and if we experience overwhelming pain.

People respond in four ways to the problems of evil and suffering. The four responses are skepticism, seeking, overcoming, and grieving. The same person may have one or more of these responses.

First, there are *skeptical* responses found in people who look at the problem of evil or personal pain and use it as a reason to question the existence of God. People with these types of responses may end up with minds bent toward agnosticism, which say, "We can't know whether God exists," or minds bent toward atheism, which say, "There is no God."

Second, there are *seeking* responses found in people who are open to hearing answers to the problem of evil. They want to pursue the issues involved and try to come to an understanding of evil and suffering in a way that makes sense or helps them.

Third, there are *overcoming* responses found in persons who accept evil and suffering as a part of life, and they work at coping with suffering when it comes. Christian overcomers continue to believe in and rely on a good, caring, and helpful God.

---

24. Vicktor E. Frankl, *Man's Search for Meaning*, (Boston, MA: Beacon Press, 1959).

Finally, fourth, there are *grieving* responses found in those who are experiencing the deep pain and hurt of losing something or someone very dear and important to them. They need comfort more than answers to the problem of evil or to their questioning of why this happened. They need freedom to express their pain and anger even toward God. Initially, it is not best to say to a grief sufferer, "God has a reason for this," for they cannot accept that kind of an answer at this time, if ever. They need people not to give them explanations and platitudes to help them feel better about what happened; they need people to come alongside them and love them by listening, accepting, and comforting them (Job 2:11-13).

There is no need to panic about friends losing their solid faith in God due to deep grief. They may question God or express anger at God, but, more than likely, they will return to their faith in due time. True faith will exhibit times of doubt but will eventually give witness to salvation in Christ Jesus. However, those with previous doubts about God or who have weak faith present great cause for concern. Hebrews is very clear that warnings of falling away need to be taken seriously. Whatever the person's faith in God, whether weak or strong, in a grieving situation, love and acceptance of their feelings is what they need rather than being dealt with about their salvation. That can come later.

God does not choose to eliminate evil and suffering from this world and our lives (Job 5:7; Romans 8:17-18), so we must choose how we will respond to our sufferings, hopefully in the most beneficial way possible. Of course, there is always the question of whether we deserve our suffering. We may or may not have a right to be angry at it. But be that as it may, the concern of all of us who find ourselves in the midst of suffering is to find a way to cope with it. Why God relieves the suffering of some of his people while others suffer unto death is not known, but faith's reward is the same for both (Hebrews 11:32-40). Our great hope is through faith in Christ (1 John 5:4). If you have ever had a miserable night and were very glad to see the morning, you can imagine the hope people of faith enjoy knowing that morning is coming. In spite of the evil, injustice, or pain, could it be that there are benefits to suffering that are good for us, thus making the experience more bearable?

What value is there in our suffering? One of my favorite illustrations comes from the caterpillar emerging from its cocoon. Someone once decided to help that process along by opening the cocoon of the butterfly to ease its struggle of trying to get out. The result was that the butterfly could not fly and died. Apparently it needed to struggle for its wings to become strong so it could fly. The Bible teaches us about many good, necessary things that can result from suffering, and you may have experienced some of them. I will share five thoughts on the value of suffering.

First, because of suffering, some are led to belief in God, or in the case of those already believing, they may be led closer to God or back to God. I suffered panic attacks and mental anguish at the thought of my death. This led me to want an answer to the question, *Is there any way for me to escape death?* This kind of suffering made me open to the gospel message, to the very words of Jesus: "He who believes in me shall never die." Trusting him and his words brought new life and peace to my troubled mind and heart. Sufferings can make us open to the need for repentance and faith lest we perish (Luke 13:1-5; 2 Corinthians 1:8-9).

Sufferings can humble us and cause us to draw near to God for help and strength (Psalm 4:1; 22:11; 119:28; Matthew 26:36-44). Many have shared how they turned to God's Word during times of suffering and found the answer they needed to enable them to go on. Those without hope can find that God alone is sufficient for their needs and wants. The psalmist recognized that God was his greatest good (Psalm 73:23-28). Perhaps that is the place we all need to get to but cannot or will not without suffering.

A second value of suffering is that it serves as a test of our hearts. Suffering reveals what is in our hearts and often our need to grow stronger. Do we have faith, love, and hope, or do we doubt, lose heart, and give up (Job 2:9-10)? Our reactions to suffering reveal who we are. They may reveal unbelief or a lack of character necessary for increased maturity or health. Through sufferings, we often are "forced" to make decisions and changes that cause us to overcome bad habits or to grow in character or faith so future sufferings are more ably endured (Psalm 119:67, 71; 2 Corinthians 12:7-10). According to the Bible, sufferings lend to the genuineness of our faith by helping to bring about perseverance and the assured hope that God's love will never fail us (Romans 5:3-5). Instead of resenting or trying to escape sufferings, we are encouraged to endure them because they help make us perfect and lacking in nothing God promises us (James 1:2-4).

Third, suffering can also help loosen our grip on the world, enabling important things of life to surface. Suffering can help us see that money, fame, material things, or self are not the important things to live for. Jesus talked to a man who had much wealth. When Jesus asked him to decide between wealth and following Jesus, he chose wealth. We can easily hold on to this world's goods more than God's goods (Mark 10:21-22). How many times have people in trouble discovered the more important things in life such as loving families, the value of friendships, appreciating the simple everyday things that happen, or enjoying the beauty of God's creation? In Jesus' story of the farmer who strove to increase his assets, Jesus reminded us that some things in life are more important than others. Life is not found in wealth or possessions (Luke 12:15–21). Without sufferings threatening to take away, or taking away, the lesser things we live for, would we ever give our efforts to living for the most worthy things?

A fourth value is that suffering helps us discover the necessity of relationships and brings us closer together. More than we may realize, we need each other to help us cope and encourage us to stay the course. Being lonely is one of the greatest sufferings imaginable. Sharing our struggles and pain with each other in our sufferings helps us realize we are not alone. I once needed a friend to listen to me regarding a life-threatening situation that had me scared and depressed. My wife was gone for a couple days, so I called another friend. He was there for me, allowed me to infringe upon his time, listened, and accepted my feelings without trying to fix me and without any attitude of condescension. By doing those things, he encouraged me immensely, and my bond of friendship with him deepened. If I can't be there like that for others, how true am I to what life is all about?

When we suffer, we are given the opportunity to love each other through our involvement in helping alleviate those sufferings. Because God works through people, experiencing the care of others helps us know that God cares and that we are not alone in this universe. Suffering also gives us opportunity to learn to be more sensitive to others and more understanding of what others may be going through (2 Corinthians 1:3-4). Through suffering, we become more accepting and loving.

Fifth, and last, suffering can show us God at work, accomplishing good that evidently could not have come about any other way. God often seems hidden and absent when we are suffering (Psalm 22:1-2; Mark 15:34). When we are able to see that he is working in ours or in others' sufferings, it encourages us to know that he cares, has not abandoned us, and is in control even in our nightmare situations. Perhaps the greatest example of this is seeing God at work in the sufferings of Jesus. Through his sufferings, we see many people are able to be saved and possess eternal life, which couldn't have happened apart from his sufferings (Isaiah 53:10-12).

In the Old Testament, Joseph suffered at the hands of his brothers by being sold into slavery, being grievously separated from his family, and being falsely accused and imprisoned in a foreign land for two years (Genesis 37, 39, 42:21). But as much as Joseph suffered, we see God working to produce unimaginable good. He saved many from starvation through his unfortunate suffering and achieved reconciliation between himself and his brothers (Genesis 50:20-21).

In Jesus' day, a man was born blind from birth. He suffered this condition in order that God could show his miraculous work and reveal Jesus as God's Son, the light of the world (John 9:1-3, 5, 35-38). Seeing God at work through people's sufferings gives us hope. When he seems absent, we should take encouragement by remembering what we have seen him do and believing he is doing something good through our suffering (Romans 8:28). He is still there, just as the sun is still there even though hidden by clouds at times.

Suffering seems necessary in a world in which evil has gotten a foothold in our lives. If it were not for suffering, we might not gain the benefits listed above. None of us likes to suffer, but efforts to escape involuntary sufferings would leave us incomplete. It seems that imperfect people, living in a world in which they are ingrained with evil and self-centeredness, need suffering to overcome the evils that plague them. Whatever can be shaken needs to be removed so what is unshakable can stand in its place (Hebrews 12:27-28).

What is acceptable and not acceptable to say about evil and suffering? It is not acceptable to say God created evil and suffering to bring about these kinds of good. In my mind, to create evil just so these kinds of values can be experienced would be inexcusable for a loving, righteous, and good God. We do not know a lot about why God allowed evil to come into the world, but since it exists, we must learn to overcome it. Evil and sufferings are never good. No! Evil causes the most painful sufferings. But we can say that through God's caring and loving power, good can come from the worst of evils (Genesis 50:20; Romans 8:28). We might say humanity's choice allowed evil into the world (Genesis 3:1-7) and that we are responsible, but God took responsibility for evil when he came in the person of his Son to suffer evil himself and to die a tortuous death in order to destroy evil and its cause (1 John 3:8; Revelation 20:10; 21:4-5).

Believers can say there is hope for the obliteration of evil and suffering sometimes in this life but completely and forever in the next. It's OK to pray for relief from suffering, but we need wisdom to know when to seek help to alleviate it in ourselves and others and when to accept it as one of God's allowed ways to enrich our lives.

A STUDY GUIDE FOR INDIVIDUALS OR GROUPS

FOR THE LEADER

The following format provides suggestions if you need ideas for leading group discussion. The same format can be used for the preface and each chapter.

Be prepared by reading the material and Bible verses and personally answering some of the discussion and application questions. This helps you add personal input into the discussion.

Choose what questions to ask the group. You may have some of your own.

As followers of Jesus, our relationships need to become deeper than just information sharing. A key purpose of the group is to get to know one another, build deeper friendships, share life stories, and develop loving support by meeting one another's needs. Allow discussion to take its natural course—it is OK to deviate from the script. Decide when to get back on task.

DISCUSSION THAT CAN APPLY TO EACH CHAPTER

1. Consider the title of the chapter. Why would you be interested, or not, in the topic?

2. Read the opening paragraph of the chapter. Share whatever thoughts come to mind.

3. Read each paragraph or section, including the scripture references. Answer any of the following questions:

   • Did anything we just read stand out or seem meaningful to you?

- What is your response to what was just read?
- What point do you think is being made (in the paragraph or Bible verses)?
- How does the verse (or verses) support or not support the point being made?
- Where do you agree or disagree?
- Do you have anything to add to the topic being discussed?
- Are there questions you have that you would like to discuss?
- Can you share any personal stories that came to mind as you read the paragraph or scriptures?
- What have you heard others you know or various media in the world say about this subject?

4. Application questions. Choose whatever ones work for you or your group, or make up your own:

- Did you learn anything new? How was this information a good reminder for you?
- How does this information benefit your life? What would it look like if you practiced this?
- What would you like to do with this information?
- If you want to put something into practice in your life, what is it, and how can others help you?
- Is there any way you can use this information to benefit your family or friends?
- How or when would be a right time to pass on some of these concepts to your kids?
- Is anyone struggling with anything involving this topic? (Be sensitive to each other's needs.)
- Can you share a time when you experienced this or did this in your life? What was the result?

www.ingramcontent.com/pod-product-compliance
Lightning Source LLC
Chambersburg PA
CBHW051738090426
42738CB00010B/2313